55 California Style Recipes for Home

By: Kelly Johnson

Table of Contents

- Avocado Toast with Poached Egg
- California Cobb Salad
- Fish Tacos with Mango Salsa
- Kale and Quinoa Salad
- Grilled Artichokes with Lemon Aioli
- California Roll Sushi Bowl
- Santa Maria-Style Tri-Tip
- Mango and Shrimp Ceviche
- California Chicken Wrap
- Quinoa Stuffed Bell Peppers
- Orange and Fennel Salad
- Grilled Vegetable Skewers
- Lemon Garlic Butter Shrimp
- California Breakfast Burrito
- Strawberry Spinach Salad
- Chicken and Avocado Quesadillas
- Pesto Pasta with Cherry Tomatoes
- California Burger with Avocado Mayo
- Asian-Inspired Salmon Bowl
- Mushroom and Goat Cheese Flatbread
- BBQ Chicken Salad
- Peach and Burrata Salad
- Zucchini Noodles with Pesto
- California Veggie Burger
- Lemon Herb Grilled Swordfish
- Sweet Potato and Black Bean Enchiladas
- Mexican Street Corn Salad
- California Caprese Skewers
- Lemon Thyme Roasted Chicken
- Teriyaki Tofu Stir-Fry
- California Rice Bowl
- Grilled Portobello Mushrooms with Pesto
- Citrus-Marinated Grilled Lamb Chops
- Mediterranean Quinoa Salad
- Spicy Sriracha Shrimp Lettuce Wraps
- California Fig and Goat Cheese Pizza

- Cilantro Lime Grilled Corn
- Tomato Basil Bruschetta
- Pomegranate Glazed Salmon
- California-Style Turkey Club
- Herb-Roasted Baby Potatoes
- Spinach and Feta Stuffed Chicken Breast
- California Sunrise Smoothie
- Miso Glazed Eggplant
- Caprese Stuffed Avocado
- Chickpea and Roasted Red Pepper Hummus Wrap
- Coconut Lime Shrimp Tacos
- California Dreaming Smoothie Bowl
- Honey-Lime Grilled Chicken Skewers
- Sesame Ginger Quinoa Bowl
- California Zoodle Salad
- Citrus Avocado Salsa
- Spaghetti Squash with Pesto and Cherry Tomatoes
- California Citrus Chicken Salad
- Mango Coconut Chia Pudding

Avocado Toast with Poached Egg

Ingredients:

- 1 ripe avocado
- 2 slices of your favorite bread (sourdough, whole grain, etc.)
- 2 large eggs
- Salt and pepper to taste
- Optional toppings: red pepper flakes, chili oil, sliced tomatoes, feta cheese, or fresh herbs like cilantro or chives

Instructions:

Toast the Bread:
- Toast the bread slices to your desired level of crispiness. You can use a toaster, toaster oven, or a regular oven.

Prepare the Avocado:
- Cut the ripe avocado in half, remove the pit, and scoop the flesh into a bowl.
- Mash the avocado with a fork until you reach your desired consistency. You can leave it slightly chunky or make it smooth.

Season the Avocado:
- Add salt and pepper to the mashed avocado, adjusting to taste. You can also add a squeeze of lemon or lime juice for a citrusy kick.

Poach the Eggs:
- Bring a small pot of water to a gentle simmer. Add a splash of vinegar to the water; this helps the egg whites coagulate more easily.
- Crack the eggs into separate bowls.
- Create a gentle whirlpool in the simmering water and slide the eggs, one at a time, into the center of the whirlpool. This helps the eggs maintain a nice shape.
- Poach the eggs for about 3-4 minutes for a runny yolk or longer if you prefer a firmer yolk.
- Carefully remove the poached eggs with a slotted spoon and place them on a paper towel to absorb excess water.

Assemble the Avocado Toast:
- Spread the mashed avocado evenly onto the toasted bread slices.
- Carefully place a poached egg on top of each slice of avocado-covered toast.

Season and Garnish:
- Sprinkle a bit of salt and pepper over the poached eggs.
- Add any optional toppings you desire, such as red pepper flakes, chili oil, sliced tomatoes, feta cheese, or fresh herbs.

Serve Immediately:
- Enjoy your delicious avocado toast with poached egg while it's warm!

This dish is not only visually appealing but also provides a satisfying combination of textures and flavors. Feel free to get creative with the toppings and customize it to your taste preferences.

California Cobb Salad

Ingredients:

For the Salad:

- 4 cups mixed salad greens (lettuce, spinach, arugula, etc.)
- 1 cup cooked and diced chicken breast
- 2 medium tomatoes, diced
- 1 large avocado, diced
- 4 hard-boiled eggs, sliced
- 6 strips of bacon, cooked and crumbled
- 1 cup crumbled blue cheese or feta cheese
- 1 cup chopped cucumber (optional)
- 1/2 cup sliced red onion (optional)

For the Dressing:

- 1/3 cup olive oil
- 2 tablespoons red wine vinegar
- 1 teaspoon Dijon mustard
- 1 clove garlic, minced
- Salt and pepper to taste

Instructions:

Prepare the Salad Base:
- In a large salad bowl, arrange the mixed salad greens as the base.

Layer the Ingredients:
- Arrange the diced chicken, tomatoes, diced avocado, sliced hard-boiled eggs, crumbled bacon, crumbled blue cheese, chopped cucumber, and sliced red onion on top of the salad greens in neat rows or sections.

Make the Dressing:
- In a small bowl, whisk together the olive oil, red wine vinegar, Dijon mustard, minced garlic, salt, and pepper until well combined. Adjust the seasoning to taste.

Drizzle the Dressing:

- Drizzle the dressing over the salad just before serving. You can use the dressing to taste, and you may not need all of it. Toss the salad gently to coat the ingredients with the dressing.

Serve:
- Serve the California Cobb Salad immediately, offering any remaining dressing on the side for those who want extra.

Feel free to customize the salad based on your preferences. You can add other ingredients like grilled corn, black beans, or different types of greens. The California Cobb Salad is not only delicious but also a well-balanced and satisfying meal. Enjoy!

Fish Tacos with Mango Salsa

Ingredients:

For the Fish Tacos:

- 1 lb white fish fillets (such as cod or tilapia)
- 1 cup all-purpose flour
- 1 teaspoon chili powder
- 1/2 teaspoon cumin
- Salt and pepper to taste
- 1 cup buttermilk
- Vegetable oil for frying
- Corn or flour tortillas

For the Mango Salsa:

- 2 ripe mangoes, peeled, pitted, and diced
- 1/2 red onion, finely diced
- 1 red bell pepper, diced
- 1/4 cup fresh cilantro, chopped
- Juice of 1 lime
- Salt and pepper to taste

For Serving:

- Shredded cabbage or lettuce
- Lime wedges
- Sour cream or Greek yogurt (optional)

Instructions:

Prepare the Mango Salsa:
- In a bowl, combine diced mangoes, red onion, red bell pepper, cilantro, lime juice, salt, and pepper. Mix well.
- Refrigerate the salsa while preparing the rest of the ingredients to allow the flavors to meld.

Prepare the Fish:
- In a shallow dish, mix the flour, chili powder, cumin, salt, and pepper.

- Dip each fish fillet into the buttermilk and then coat it with the seasoned flour mixture, ensuring an even coating.

Fry the Fish:
- Heat vegetable oil in a skillet over medium-high heat.
- Fry the coated fish fillets for 3-4 minutes per side or until golden brown and cooked through.
- Place the fried fish on a paper towel to absorb any excess oil.

Warm the Tortillas:
- Heat the tortillas in a dry skillet or warm them in the oven according to package instructions.

Assemble the Tacos:
- Place a portion of the fried fish in each tortilla.
- Top with shredded cabbage or lettuce.
- Spoon mango salsa over the fish.
- Add a dollop of sour cream or Greek yogurt if desired.

Serve:
- Serve the fish tacos with mango salsa immediately, garnished with lime wedges on the side.

These fish tacos with mango salsa are not only delicious but also customizable to suit your taste. Feel free to add additional toppings such as sliced radishes, jalapeños, or your favorite hot sauce for an extra kick. Enjoy your flavorful and refreshing meal!

Kale and Quinoa Salad

Ingredients:

For the Salad:

- 1 cup quinoa, rinsed
- 2 cups water or vegetable broth
- 1 bunch of kale, stems removed and leaves chopped
- 1 cup cherry tomatoes, halved
- 1 cucumber, diced
- 1/2 red onion, finely chopped
- 1/2 cup feta cheese, crumbled (optional)
- 1/4 cup sunflower seeds or pumpkin seeds (optional)

For the Dressing:

- 1/4 cup extra-virgin olive oil
- 2 tablespoons balsamic vinegar
- 1 tablespoon Dijon mustard
- 1 clove garlic, minced
- Salt and pepper to taste

Instructions:

Cook Quinoa:
- In a medium saucepan, combine quinoa and water or vegetable broth. Bring to a boil, then reduce heat to low, cover, and simmer for about 15 minutes or until the quinoa is cooked and water is absorbed.
- Remove from heat and let it sit, covered, for 5 minutes. Fluff the quinoa with a fork and allow it to cool.

Massage the Kale:
- In a large bowl, place the chopped kale. Massage the kale with your hands for a few minutes to soften it and make it more palatable.

Assemble the Salad:
- Add the cooled quinoa, cherry tomatoes, cucumber, red onion, and feta cheese (if using) to the bowl with the massaged kale.

Prepare the Dressing:
- In a small bowl, whisk together the olive oil, balsamic vinegar, Dijon mustard, minced garlic, salt, and pepper until well combined.

Toss and Coat:
- Drizzle the dressing over the salad and toss everything together until well coated.

Optional Additions:
- Sprinkle sunflower seeds or pumpkin seeds on top for added crunch and nutritional value.

Chill and Serve:
- Refrigerate the salad for at least 30 minutes before serving to allow the flavors to meld.

Serve:
- Serve the kale and quinoa salad chilled, and enjoy as a refreshing and nutritious meal.

This kale and quinoa salad is versatile, and you can customize it by adding your favorite veggies, nuts, or protein sources. It's a great option for a light lunch or a side dish with dinner.

Grilled Artichokes with Lemon Aioli

Ingredients:

For Grilled Artichokes:

- 4 large artichokes
- 2 lemons, halved
- Olive oil
- Salt and pepper to taste

For Lemon Aioli:

- 1 cup mayonnaise
- 2 cloves garlic, minced
- Zest of 1 lemon
- 2 tablespoons fresh lemon juice
- 1 teaspoon Dijon mustard
- Salt and pepper to taste

Instructions:

Grilled Artichokes:

Prepare Artichokes:
- Trim the tough outer leaves of the artichokes. Cut off the top inch of each artichoke and trim the stem, leaving about 1 inch.
- Cut the artichokes in half lengthwise.

Remove Choke:
- Use a spoon to scoop out the fuzzy choke from the center of each artichoke half.

Precook Artichokes:
- Place the artichokes in a large pot of salted boiling water with lemon halves for about 15-20 minutes, or until they are slightly tender.

Drain and Season:
- Drain the artichokes and brush them with olive oil. Season with salt and pepper.

Grill Artichokes:
- Preheat the grill to medium-high heat. Grill the artichokes, cut side down, for 5-7 minutes or until they develop grill marks. Flip and grill for an additional 5-7 minutes.

Serve:
- Remove the grilled artichokes from the grill and squeeze fresh lemon juice over them before serving.

Lemon Aioli:

Prepare Aioli:
- In a small bowl, combine mayonnaise, minced garlic, lemon zest, lemon juice, Dijon mustard, salt, and pepper.

Mix Well:
- Whisk the ingredients together until well combined. Adjust the seasoning to taste.

Chill:
- Refrigerate the lemon aioli for at least 30 minutes to allow the flavors to meld.

Serve:
- Serve the grilled artichokes with the chilled lemon aioli on the side for dipping.

These grilled artichokes with lemon aioli are a fantastic appetizer or side dish, perfect for sharing with friends and family. The combination of smoky, charred artichokes and the zesty aioli is sure to be a hit at your next gathering. Enjoy!

California Roll Sushi Bowl

Ingredients:

For the Sushi Bowl:

- 2 cups sushi rice, cooked and seasoned with rice vinegar, sugar, and salt
- 1 cup imitation crab or real crab, shredded
- 1 ripe avocado, sliced
- 1 cucumber, julienned
- 1/4 cup pickled ginger
- 2 tablespoons sesame seeds (black or white), toasted
- Nori sheets, cut into thin strips or small squares

For the Sauce:

- 1/4 cup mayonnaise
- 1 tablespoon soy sauce
- 1 teaspoon sriracha (optional, for a spicy kick)

Optional Garnishes:

- Sliced green onions
- Soy sauce or tamari for drizzling
- Wasabi and/or pickled radish for extra flavor

Instructions:

Prepare Sushi Rice:
- Cook sushi rice according to package instructions and season with rice vinegar, sugar, and salt. Allow it to cool.

Prepare Sauce:
- In a small bowl, mix together mayonnaise, soy sauce, and sriracha (if using). Adjust the quantities to taste.

Assemble the Sushi Bowl:
- In individual bowls or a larger serving bowl, arrange a portion of the sushi rice as the base.

Add Toppings:
- Top the rice with shredded crab, sliced avocado, julienned cucumber, pickled ginger, and toasted sesame seeds.

Drizzle with Sauce:
- Drizzle the sauce over the toppings or serve it on the side.

Garnish:
- Garnish the California Roll Sushi Bowl with nori strips, sliced green onions, and any optional garnishes you prefer.

Serve:
- Serve the sushi bowl immediately, and if desired, offer additional soy sauce or tamari, wasabi, and pickled radish on the side.

Enjoy the flavors of a California roll in a convenient and customizable sushi bowl format.

This dish allows you to personalize the ingredients and ratios based on your

preferences, making it a versatile and delicious option for a quick and satisfying meal.

Santa Maria-Style Tri-Tip

Ingredients:

For the Tri-Tip:

- 1 whole tri-tip roast (approximately 2 to 3 pounds)
- Santa Maria-style seasoning rub (recipe below)

Santa Maria-Style Seasoning Rub:

- 2 tablespoons kosher salt
- 1 tablespoon black pepper, freshly ground
- 1 tablespoon garlic powder
- 1 tablespoon onion powder
- 1 teaspoon paprika
- 1 teaspoon dried oregano

For Serving (Optional):

- Salsa or pico de gallo
- Chimichurri sauce
- Grilled vegetables
- Garlic bread or rolls

Instructions:

Prepare the Seasoning Rub:
- In a small bowl, mix together the kosher salt, black pepper, garlic powder, onion powder, paprika, and dried oregano to create the Santa Maria-style seasoning rub.

Season the Tri-Tip:
- Pat the tri-tip dry with paper towels. Rub the seasoning mixture generously over the entire surface of the tri-tip. Ensure that the seasoning adheres well to the meat.

Marinate (Optional):
- For added flavor, you can let the seasoned tri-tip marinate in the refrigerator for at least 1-2 hours, or even overnight.

Preheat the Grill:

- Preheat your grill to medium-high heat. The Santa Maria-style tri-tip is traditionally cooked over red oak wood, but you can use charcoal or gas as well.

Grill the Tri-Tip:
- Place the seasoned tri-tip on the preheated grill and sear each side for about 5-7 minutes to create a flavorful crust.

Adjust Heat and Cook to Desired Doneness:
- After searing, move the tri-tip to a cooler part of the grill or reduce the heat. Continue cooking, turning occasionally, until the internal temperature reaches your desired doneness. For medium-rare, aim for an internal temperature of around 130-135°F (54-57°C).

Rest the Tri-Tip:
- Once cooked to your liking, remove the tri-tip from the grill and let it rest for about 10 minutes. This allows the juices to redistribute and ensures a juicy and tender result.

Slice and Serve:
- Slice the tri-tip against the grain into thin slices. Serve with your choice of accompaniments such as salsa, chimichurri sauce, grilled vegetables, or garlic bread.

Santa Maria-style tri-tip is known for its robust flavor and tenderness. Whether you're hosting a barbecue or just want to enjoy a tasty grilled dish, this recipe is sure to impress.

Mango and Shrimp Ceviche

Ingredients:

- 1 pound raw shrimp, peeled, deveined, and chopped into bite-sized pieces
- 2 ripe mangoes, peeled, pitted, and diced
- 1 red onion, finely chopped
- 1 cucumber, diced
- 1-2 jalapeños, seeded and finely chopped (adjust to taste)
- 1/2 cup fresh cilantro, chopped
- Juice of 4-5 limes
- Salt and pepper to taste
- Tortilla chips or tostadas for serving

Instructions:

Cook the Shrimp:
- Bring a pot of salted water to a boil. Add the chopped shrimp and cook for 2-3 minutes or until they turn pink and opaque. Drain the shrimp and transfer them to a bowl of ice water to cool quickly.

Prepare Mango and Vegetables:
- In a large bowl, combine the diced mangoes, chopped red onion, diced cucumber, jalapeños, and cilantro.

Finish Shrimp:
- Once the shrimp are cooled, drain them and add them to the bowl with the mango and vegetables.

Add Lime Juice:
- Squeeze the juice of 4-5 limes over the mixture. Adjust the amount of lime juice based on your preference.

Season:
- Season the ceviche with salt and pepper to taste. Mix everything well to ensure the ingredients are evenly coated with lime juice.

Chill:
- Cover the ceviche with plastic wrap and refrigerate for at least 30 minutes to allow the flavors to meld and the shrimp to marinate in the lime juice.

Serve:
- Once chilled, give the ceviche a final stir and serve it in bowls or on tostadas. You can also serve it with tortilla chips on the side.

Enjoy this mango and shrimp ceviche as a refreshing and vibrant dish. The combination of sweet mango, succulent shrimp, and the citrusy kick from lime creates a delightful mix of flavors. It's perfect for summer gatherings or any occasion where you want a light and delicious appetizer.

California Chicken Wrap

Ingredients:

For the Grilled Chicken:

- 2 boneless, skinless chicken breasts
- 2 tablespoons olive oil
- 1 teaspoon garlic powder
- 1 teaspoon cumin
- Salt and pepper to taste

For the Wrap Assembly:

- Large flour tortillas or wraps
- 1 avocado, sliced
- 1 cup cherry tomatoes, halved
- 1 cup shredded lettuce
- 1/2 cup shredded cheese (cheddar, Monterey Jack, or your choice)
- 1/4 cup red onion, thinly sliced
- 1/4 cup cilantro, chopped
- Optional: Salsa, sour cream, or your favorite dressing for drizzling

Instructions:

Grill the Chicken:
- In a bowl, mix olive oil, garlic powder, cumin, salt, and pepper to create a marinade.
- Coat the chicken breasts with the marinade and let them marinate for at least 30 minutes.
- Preheat a grill or grill pan over medium-high heat.
- Grill the chicken breasts for 6-8 minutes per side or until fully cooked (internal temperature reaches 165°F or 74°C).
- Allow the chicken to rest for a few minutes before slicing it into thin strips.

Prepare the Wrap Ingredients:
- Slice the avocado, halve the cherry tomatoes, shred the lettuce, and prepare the other ingredients for assembly.

Assemble the Wraps:
- Warm the tortillas briefly in a dry skillet or microwave.

- Place a tortilla on a clean surface and arrange a portion of sliced grilled chicken down the center.

Add Fresh Ingredients:
- Layer the sliced avocado, halved cherry tomatoes, shredded lettuce, shredded cheese, sliced red onion, and chopped cilantro on top of the chicken.

Drizzle with Dressing (Optional):
- Drizzle salsa, sour cream, or your favorite dressing over the ingredients.

Wrap it Up:
- Fold in the sides of the tortilla and then roll it up tightly from the bottom to create the wrap.

Serve:
- Cut the wrap in half diagonally and serve immediately.

These California Chicken Wraps are not only delicious but also versatile. Feel free to customize them with additional ingredients like black beans, corn, or bell peppers. They make for a quick and satisfying lunch or dinner, and the combination of grilled chicken and fresh vegetables provides a delightful burst of flavors.

Quinoa Stuffed Bell Peppers

Ingredients:

- 4 large bell peppers (any color)
- 1 cup quinoa, rinsed
- 2 cups vegetable broth or water
- 1 tablespoon olive oil
- 1 onion, finely chopped
- 2 cloves garlic, minced
- 1 zucchini, diced
- 1 carrot, grated
- 1 cup black beans, drained and rinsed
- 1 cup corn kernels (fresh, frozen, or canned)
- 1 teaspoon cumin
- 1 teaspoon chili powder
- Salt and pepper to taste
- 1 cup shredded cheese (cheddar, Monterey Jack, or your choice)
- Fresh cilantro or parsley for garnish (optional)

Instructions:

Preheat the Oven:
- Preheat your oven to 375°F (190°C).

Prepare Quinoa:
- In a medium saucepan, combine quinoa and vegetable broth or water. Bring to a boil, then reduce heat to low, cover, and simmer for about 15 minutes or until the quinoa is cooked and liquid is absorbed. Fluff the quinoa with a fork and set aside.

Prepare Bell Peppers:
- Cut the tops off the bell peppers and remove the seeds and membranes. If needed, trim the bottoms slightly to help them stand upright in the baking dish.

Sauté Vegetables:
- In a large skillet, heat olive oil over medium heat. Add chopped onions and garlic, sautéing until softened.
- Add diced zucchini, grated carrot, black beans, and corn. Cook for an additional 3-5 minutes until the vegetables are tender.

Season:
- Add cumin, chili powder, salt, and pepper to the vegetable mixture. Stir well to combine.

Combine Quinoa and Vegetables:
- In a large bowl, mix the cooked quinoa with the sautéed vegetable mixture until well combined.

Stuff the Peppers:
- Stuff each bell pepper with the quinoa and vegetable mixture, pressing it down gently.

Top with Cheese:
- Sprinkle shredded cheese over the top of each stuffed pepper.

Bake:
- Place the stuffed peppers in a baking dish and bake in the preheated oven for about 25-30 minutes or until the peppers are tender, and the cheese is melted and bubbly.

Garnish and Serve:
- Garnish with fresh cilantro or parsley if desired. Serve the quinoa stuffed bell peppers hot.

These quinoa stuffed bell peppers are a wholesome and satisfying meal. Feel free to customize the filling with your favorite vegetables, spices, or protein sources. They make for a delicious and colorful dish that's perfect for a healthy lunch or dinner.

Orange and Fennel Salad

Ingredients:

- 3 medium-sized oranges (navel oranges or blood oranges work well)
- 1 medium fennel bulb, thinly sliced
- 1/4 cup red onion, thinly sliced
- 1/4 cup fresh parsley, chopped
- 2 tablespoons extra-virgin olive oil
- 1 tablespoon red wine vinegar or white balsamic vinegar
- Salt and pepper to taste
- Optional: Fennel fronds for garnish

Instructions:

Prepare Oranges:
- Using a sharp knife, cut off the tops and bottoms of the oranges to reveal the flesh. Place one orange flat on a cutting board and carefully cut away the peel and white pith, following the curve of the orange. Repeat for all oranges.
- Hold each peeled orange over a bowl and cut along both sides of each segment to release them. Repeat for all oranges, collecting the juice in the bowl.

Assemble the Salad:
- In a large bowl, combine the sliced fennel, red onion, and orange segments.

Make the Dressing:
- In a small bowl, whisk together the olive oil, red wine vinegar or white balsamic vinegar, and a pinch of salt and pepper. If you have collected orange juice while segmenting, you can add a tablespoon or two to the dressing for extra citrus flavor.

Toss and Coat:
- Drizzle the dressing over the salad and toss everything together until the ingredients are evenly coated.

Garnish:
- Sprinkle fresh parsley over the salad and toss again to distribute evenly. Optionally, garnish with fennel fronds for added flavor and presentation.

Chill (Optional):

- You can refrigerate the salad for 30 minutes to allow the flavors to meld and the salad to cool slightly before serving.

Serve:
- Serve the orange and fennel salad on a platter or individual plates. Enjoy the crisp, citrusy goodness!

This salad is not only a beautiful addition to any meal but also a great palate cleanser. The combination of sweet oranges, crunchy fennel, and the zesty dressing creates a harmonious and refreshing dish. It's perfect for light lunches, as a side dish, or as a refreshing salad during warm weather.

Grilled Vegetable Skewers

Ingredients:

- Assorted vegetables (choose a mix of colors and textures):
    - Cherry tomatoes
    - Bell peppers (various colors)
    - Zucchini
    - Yellow squash
    - Red onion
    - Mushrooms
    - Eggplant
- Olive oil
- Balsamic vinegar (optional)
- Garlic, minced
- Fresh herbs (such as rosemary, thyme, or oregano), chopped
- Salt and pepper to taste
- Wooden or metal skewers

Instructions:

Prepare the Skewers:
- If you're using wooden skewers, soak them in water for about 30 minutes to prevent burning during grilling.
- Cut the vegetables into bite-sized pieces, ensuring they are relatively uniform in size for even cooking.

Marinate the Vegetables:
- In a bowl, whisk together olive oil, balsamic vinegar (if using), minced garlic, chopped fresh herbs, salt, and pepper. Adjust the quantities to your taste.
- Toss the cut vegetables in the marinade, ensuring they are well-coated. Allow them to marinate for at least 15-30 minutes to absorb the flavors.

Assemble the Skewers:
- Thread the marinated vegetables onto the skewers, alternating the different types and colors of vegetables.

Preheat the Grill:
- Preheat your grill to medium-high heat.

Grill the Skewers:

- Place the vegetable skewers on the preheated grill. Grill for about 10-15 minutes, turning occasionally, until the vegetables are tender and slightly charred.

Serve:
- Remove the skewers from the grill and place them on a serving platter.
- Optionally, drizzle with a little extra olive oil or balsamic vinegar before serving.

Garnish (Optional):
- Garnish the grilled vegetable skewers with additional chopped fresh herbs for a burst of flavor.

Enjoy:
- Serve the grilled vegetable skewers as a side dish or a main course. They pair well with various sauces or dips like tzatziki or balsamic reduction.

These grilled vegetable skewers are not only visually appealing but also packed with smoky, grilled goodness. Feel free to customize the vegetable selection and marinade to suit your preferences. They're a fantastic option for a vegetarian barbecue or a flavorful side dish to complement your main course.

Lemon Garlic Butter Shrimp

Ingredients:

- 1 pound large shrimp, peeled and deveined
- 3 tablespoons unsalted butter
- 4 cloves garlic, minced
- 1/2 cup chicken broth or white wine
- Juice of 1 lemon (about 2 tablespoons)
- Zest of 1 lemon
- 1 teaspoon dried oregano or thyme
- Salt and black pepper to taste
- Crushed red pepper flakes (optional, for a bit of heat)
- Fresh parsley, chopped, for garnish
- Cooked pasta, rice, or crusty bread for serving

Instructions:

Prepare Shrimp:
- Pat the shrimp dry with paper towels and season with salt and black pepper.

Cook Shrimp:
- In a large skillet over medium-high heat, melt 2 tablespoons of butter. Add the shrimp to the skillet and cook for 1-2 minutes per side or until they turn pink and opaque. Remove the shrimp from the skillet and set aside.

Make Lemon Garlic Butter Sauce:
- In the same skillet, add the remaining 1 tablespoon of butter. Add minced garlic and sauté for about 30 seconds until fragrant but not browned.

Deglaze the Pan:
- Pour in the chicken broth or white wine, scraping the bottom of the pan to deglaze it. Allow it to simmer for 2-3 minutes to reduce slightly.

Add Lemon Juice and Zest:
- Stir in the lemon juice and lemon zest, and add dried oregano or thyme. Mix well to combine.

Return Shrimp to Skillet:
- Return the cooked shrimp to the skillet, tossing them in the lemon garlic butter sauce until well coated. If desired, add crushed red pepper flakes for a bit of heat.

Season and Garnish:
- Taste the sauce and adjust the seasoning with salt and black pepper as needed. Sprinkle fresh chopped parsley over the shrimp.

Serve:
- Serve the lemon garlic butter shrimp over cooked pasta, rice, or with crusty bread to soak up the flavorful sauce.

This lemon garlic butter shrimp recipe is both quick and versatile. You can easily adjust the flavors and serve it with your favorite side dishes. It's a delightful combination of citrusy, garlicky, and buttery goodness that will surely become a favorite in your repertoire.

California Breakfast Burrito

Ingredients:

- 4 large flour tortillas
- 6 large eggs
- 1 tablespoon butter or cooking oil
- Salt and pepper to taste
- 1 cup shredded cheddar or Monterey Jack cheese
- 1 cup cooked and diced breakfast potatoes
- 1 cup cooked and crumbled breakfast sausage or bacon
- 1 ripe avocado, sliced
- Salsa or hot sauce for serving
- Fresh cilantro or green onions for garnish (optional)

Instructions:

Cook the Eggs:
- In a bowl, whisk the eggs and season with salt and pepper.
- Heat butter or oil in a skillet over medium heat. Pour the whisked eggs into the skillet and scramble until cooked through.

Assemble the Burritos:
- Warm the flour tortillas in a dry skillet or microwave to make them pliable.
- Lay out each tortilla and distribute the scrambled eggs evenly down the center.

Add Fillings:
- Layer on the shredded cheese, cooked breakfast potatoes, and crumbled breakfast sausage or bacon.

Add Avocado:
- Place slices of ripe avocado on top of the other fillings.

Fold and Roll:
- Fold in the sides of the tortilla and then roll it up tightly from the bottom to create the burrito.

Heat (Optional):
- If desired, you can heat the assembled burritos in a skillet for a minute or two on each side to melt the cheese and warm the fillings.

Serve:

- Serve the California breakfast burritos with salsa or hot sauce on the side. Garnish with fresh cilantro or green onions if desired.

Enjoy these hearty and flavorful California breakfast burritos as a satisfying morning meal. You can customize the fillings based on your preferences, adding ingredients like black beans, pico de gallo, or sautéed vegetables for extra flavor. They are perfect for breakfast on the go or a leisurely weekend brunch.

Strawberry Spinach Salad

Ingredients:

For the Salad:

- 6 cups fresh baby spinach leaves, washed and dried
- 2 cups strawberries, hulled and sliced
- 1/2 cup feta cheese, crumbled
- 1/4 cup red onion, thinly sliced
- 1/4 cup sliced almonds or candied pecans

For the Dressing:

- 3 tablespoons balsamic vinegar
- 2 tablespoons extra-virgin olive oil
- 1 tablespoon honey
- 1 teaspoon Dijon mustard
- Salt and pepper to taste

Instructions:

Prepare the Salad:
- In a large salad bowl, combine the fresh spinach leaves, sliced strawberries, crumbled feta cheese, thinly sliced red onion, and sliced almonds or candied pecans.

Make the Dressing:
- In a small bowl or jar, whisk together balsamic vinegar, olive oil, honey, Dijon mustard, salt, and pepper. Adjust the quantities to your taste.

Toss the Salad:
- Drizzle the dressing over the salad and toss gently to coat the ingredients evenly.

Serve:
- Serve the Strawberry Spinach Salad immediately, ensuring that each serving has a good mix of spinach, strawberries, feta, and nuts.

Optional Additions:
- Customize your salad by adding grilled chicken or shrimp for a protein boost.
- Consider adding avocado slices for extra creaminess.

Garnish (Optional):
- Garnish with additional sliced strawberries, crumbled feta, or fresh herbs for a decorative touch.

This Strawberry Spinach Salad is not only visually appealing but also a perfect balance of sweet and savory flavors. The combination of fresh spinach and ripe strawberries creates a refreshing and nutritious dish. It's an excellent side salad for a variety of meals or a light and satisfying main course for a warm day.

Chicken and Avocado Quesadillas

Ingredients:

- 2 cups cooked and shredded chicken breast
- 1 teaspoon chili powder
- 1/2 teaspoon cumin
- 1/2 teaspoon garlic powder
- Salt and pepper to taste
- 4 large flour tortillas
- 1 cup shredded cheese (cheddar, Monterey Jack, or a blend)
- 1 ripe avocado, sliced
- Salsa, sour cream, or guacamole for serving
- Fresh cilantro, chopped, for garnish (optional)
- Lime wedges for serving

Instructions:

Season the Chicken:
- In a bowl, combine the shredded chicken with chili powder, cumin, garlic powder, salt, and pepper. Mix well to evenly coat the chicken.

Assemble the Quesadillas:
- Lay out the flour tortillas on a clean surface. Divide the seasoned chicken among the tortillas, spreading it evenly over half of each tortilla.

Add Avocado and Cheese:
- Place avocado slices on top of the chicken, and sprinkle shredded cheese over the avocado.

Fold and Press:
- Fold the tortillas in half over the filling, creating half-moon shapes. Press them down gently.

Cook on a Skillet:
- Heat a large skillet or griddle over medium heat. Place the filled tortillas on the skillet and cook for 2-3 minutes per side or until the tortillas are crispy and the cheese is melted.

Serve:
- Remove the quesadillas from the skillet and cut them into wedges. Serve them hot with salsa, sour cream, guacamole, or your favorite dipping sauce.

Garnish (Optional):

- Garnish with chopped fresh cilantro and serve with lime wedges on the side for squeezing over the quesadillas.

These chicken and avocado quesadillas are a crowd-pleaser and can be customized with additional ingredients like diced tomatoes, black beans, or corn. They make for a quick and flavorful meal that's great for lunch, dinner, or even as a party appetizer. Enjoy the combination of the creamy avocado, seasoned chicken, and gooey melted cheese in every bite!

Pesto Pasta with Cherry Tomatoes

Ingredients:

- 8 oz (about 225g) pasta of your choice (e.g., spaghetti, fettuccine, or penne)
- 1 cup fresh basil leaves, packed
- 1/2 cup grated Parmesan cheese
- 1/4 cup pine nuts or walnuts (optional)
- 2 cloves garlic, peeled
- 1/2 cup extra-virgin olive oil
- Salt and pepper to taste
- 1 pint (about 2 cups) cherry tomatoes, halved
- Additional grated Parmesan for serving (optional)

Instructions:

Cook the Pasta:
- Cook the pasta according to the package instructions in a large pot of salted boiling water until al dente. Reserve about 1/2 cup of pasta cooking water before draining.

Prepare the Pesto:
- In a food processor, combine the fresh basil, grated Parmesan cheese, pine nuts or walnuts (if using), and garlic cloves. Pulse until the ingredients are finely chopped.

Add Olive Oil:
- With the food processor running, slowly pour in the extra-virgin olive oil until the pesto reaches a smooth consistency. If needed, stop and scrape down the sides with a spatula.

Season:
- Season the pesto with salt and pepper to taste. Adjust the quantities according to your preference.

Combine Pasta and Pesto:
- In a large mixing bowl, toss the cooked and drained pasta with the freshly made pesto. If the pesto is too thick, you can add a bit of the reserved pasta cooking water to achieve the desired consistency.

Add Cherry Tomatoes:
- Gently fold in the halved cherry tomatoes, distributing them evenly throughout the pasta.

Serve:
- Serve the pesto pasta with cherry tomatoes on individual plates or in a serving bowl. Optionally, sprinkle additional grated Parmesan cheese on top before serving.

Garnish (Optional):
- Garnish with a few fresh basil leaves for a decorative touch.

This pesto pasta with cherry tomatoes is a light and flavorful dish that comes together quickly. It's perfect for a fresh and satisfying meal, especially during the warmer months when tomatoes and basil are in season. Enjoy the burst of flavors from the pesto and the sweetness of the cherry tomatoes!

California Burger with Avocado Mayo

Ingredients:

For the Burger Patties:

- 1 pound ground beef (or your choice of ground meat)
- Salt and pepper to taste
- 4 burger buns

For the Avocado Mayo:

- 2 ripe avocados, peeled and pitted
- 1/4 cup mayonnaise
- 1 clove garlic, minced
- 1 tablespoon lime or lemon juice
- Salt and pepper to taste

Toppings:

- Lettuce leaves
- Tomato slices
- Red onion slices
- Cheese slices (cheddar, Monterey Jack, or your favorite)
- Pickles (optional)

Instructions:

Preheat the Grill or Stovetop Griddle:
- Preheat your grill or stovetop griddle to medium-high heat.

Season and Form Burger Patties:
- Season the ground beef with salt and pepper. Divide it into 4 equal portions and shape them into burger patties.

Grill the Burger Patties:
- Place the burger patties on the preheated grill or griddle. Cook for about 4-5 minutes per side, or until they reach your desired level of doneness. Add cheese slices during the last minute of cooking to melt them.

Prepare Avocado Mayo:
- In a bowl, mash the ripe avocados. Add mayonnaise, minced garlic, lime or lemon juice, salt, and pepper. Mix until well combined. Adjust seasoning to taste.

Toast Burger Buns:
- While the burger patties are cooking, lightly toast the burger buns on the grill or in a toaster.

Assemble the Burgers:
- Spread a generous amount of avocado mayo on the bottom half of each toasted bun.
- Place a grilled burger patty on top of the mayo-covered bun.
- Layer with lettuce leaves, tomato slices, red onion slices, and pickles (if using).

Top and Serve:
- Place the top half of the bun over the toppings, securing the burger.
- Repeat for the remaining burgers.

Serve Immediately:
- Serve the California burgers with avocado mayo immediately, and enjoy the fresh and creamy flavors.

These California burgers with avocado mayo are a tasty and satisfying meal. The creamy avocado mayo adds a delicious twist to the classic burger, making it a perfect option for those who love the flavors of California cuisine. Customize the toppings to suit your preferences, and feel free to add other ingredients like bacon or sprouts for extra flavor and texture.

Asian-Inspired Salmon Bowl

Ingredients:

For the Salmon:

- 4 salmon fillets (about 6 oz each)
- 3 tablespoons soy sauce
- 2 tablespoons honey
- 1 tablespoon rice vinegar
- 1 tablespoon sesame oil
- 1 tablespoon grated ginger
- 2 cloves garlic, minced
- Sesame seeds for garnish (optional)

For the Bowl:

- 2 cups cooked brown rice or quinoa
- 2 cups broccoli florets, steamed
- 1 large carrot, julienned
- 1 cucumber, sliced
- 1 avocado, sliced
- Green onions, chopped, for garnish
- Fresh cilantro or parsley, chopped, for garnish
- Lime wedges for serving

Instructions:

Marinate and Cook the Salmon:
- In a bowl, whisk together soy sauce, honey, rice vinegar, sesame oil, grated ginger, and minced garlic to create the marinade.
- Place the salmon fillets in a shallow dish and pour half of the marinade over them. Allow the salmon to marinate for at least 15 minutes.
- Preheat the oven to 400°F (200°C). Place the marinated salmon fillets on a baking sheet lined with parchment paper. Bake for 12-15 minutes or until the salmon is cooked through.

Prepare the Rice/Quinoa and Vegetables:

- Cook the brown rice or quinoa according to the package instructions.
- Steam the broccoli florets until tender-crisp.

Assemble the Bowl:
- In each serving bowl, place a portion of cooked rice or quinoa.
- Top with steamed broccoli, julienned carrot, cucumber slices, and avocado slices.

Place Salmon on Top:
- Once the salmon is done baking, place a salmon fillet on top of each bowl.

Drizzle with Sauce:
- Drizzle the remaining marinade over the salmon and vegetables in each bowl.

Garnish:
- Garnish the bowls with chopped green onions, sesame seeds (if desired), and fresh cilantro or parsley.

Serve with Lime Wedges:
- Serve the Asian-inspired salmon bowls with lime wedges on the side for squeezing over the dish.

Enjoy your delicious and nutritious Asian-inspired salmon bowl! Feel free to customize the bowl with your favorite vegetables or add a drizzle of sriracha for some heat.

Mushroom and Goat Cheese Flatbread

Ingredients:

For the Flatbread:

- 1 pre-made flatbread or pizza crust
- 2 tablespoons olive oil
- 2 cloves garlic, minced
- Salt and black pepper to taste

For the Toppings:

- 1 cup mushrooms, thinly sliced (a mix of cremini and shiitake works well)
- 1 tablespoon olive oil
- Salt and black pepper to taste
- 4 oz (about 1/2 cup) goat cheese, crumbled
- 2 tablespoons fresh thyme leaves
- Balsamic glaze for drizzling (optional)

Instructions:

Preheat the Oven:
- Preheat your oven according to the instructions on the flatbread or pizza crust package.

Prepare the Mushroom Toppings:
- In a skillet, heat 1 tablespoon of olive oil over medium heat. Add the sliced mushrooms, and sauté until they are tender and any released liquid has evaporated. Season with salt and black pepper to taste. Set aside.

Prepare the Flatbread:
- In a small bowl, mix 2 tablespoons of olive oil with minced garlic, salt, and black pepper. Brush this mixture over the flatbread.

Assemble the Flatbread:
- Spread the sautéed mushrooms evenly over the flatbread.
- Sprinkle crumbled goat cheese on top.
- Scatter fresh thyme leaves over the mushrooms and goat cheese.

Bake:

- Place the assembled flatbread on a baking sheet or pizza stone. Follow the baking instructions on the flatbread or pizza crust package. Bake until the crust is golden and the toppings are bubbly and slightly browned.

Finish and Serve:
- Once out of the oven, drizzle balsamic glaze over the flatbread if desired.
- Slice and serve immediately.

Enjoy your delicious mushroom and goat cheese flatbread! The combination of earthy mushrooms, creamy goat cheese, and aromatic thyme creates a delightful flavor profile. This flatbread is versatile, and you can add arugula, spinach, or a balsamic reduction for extra freshness and depth of flavor.

BBQ Chicken Salad

Ingredients:

For the BBQ Chicken:

- 2 boneless, skinless chicken breasts
- 1 cup barbecue sauce
- 1 tablespoon olive oil
- Salt and pepper to taste
- 1 teaspoon smoked paprika (optional for extra smokiness)

For the Salad:

- 8 cups mixed salad greens (lettuce, spinach, arugula, etc.)
- 1 cup cherry tomatoes, halved
- 1 cup corn kernels (fresh, frozen, or canned)
- 1 cup black beans, drained and rinsed
- 1 red onion, thinly sliced
- 1 avocado, sliced
- 1/2 cup shredded cheddar cheese (optional)
- Ranch dressing or your favorite dressing for serving

Instructions:

Preheat the Grill or Oven:
- Preheat your grill or oven to medium-high heat.

Prepare the BBQ Chicken:
- Season the chicken breasts with salt, pepper, and smoked paprika.
- Brush the chicken breasts with olive oil.
- Grill the chicken for 6-8 minutes per side or until fully cooked. Alternatively, you can bake them in the oven at 400°F (200°C) for about 20-25 minutes or until done.
- During the last few minutes of cooking, baste the chicken with barbecue sauce, turning and basting until the sauce caramelizes.

Slice the Chicken:

- Let the grilled chicken rest for a few minutes, then slice it into strips or cubes.

Assemble the Salad:
- In a large salad bowl, combine the mixed greens, cherry tomatoes, corn, black beans, red onion, and avocado slices.

Add BBQ Chicken:
- Place the sliced BBQ chicken on top of the salad.

Optional Toppings:
- Sprinkle shredded cheddar cheese over the salad if desired.

Serve:
- Drizzle ranch dressing or your favorite dressing over the salad just before serving.

Toss and Enjoy:
- Toss the salad gently to combine all the ingredients, ensuring the barbecue chicken is evenly distributed.

Serve the BBQ chicken salad immediately, and enjoy the combination of smoky chicken, fresh vegetables, and the tangy goodness of barbecue sauce. Feel free to customize the salad with additional toppings like crispy bacon, croutons, or sliced jalapeños for extra flavor and texture.

Peach and Burrata Salad

Ingredients:

- 3 ripe peaches, sliced
- 1 ball of burrata cheese
- Handful of fresh basil leaves
- Handful of fresh mint leaves
- 2 tablespoons extra-virgin olive oil
- 1 tablespoon balsamic glaze
- Salt and black pepper to taste
- Optional: Prosciutto slices for garnish

Instructions:

Prepare the Peaches:
- Wash and slice the peaches into thin wedges. If the peaches are ripe, the skin should be easy to peel off.

Assemble the Salad:
- Arrange the peach slices on a serving platter or individual plates.

Add Burrata:
- Tear the burrata cheese into pieces and scatter them over the peaches.

Add Fresh Herbs:
- Sprinkle fresh basil and mint leaves over the salad.

Drizzle with Olive Oil and Balsamic Glaze:
- Drizzle extra-virgin olive oil and balsamic glaze over the salad.

Season:
- Season with a pinch of salt and black pepper to taste.

Optional: Garnish with Prosciutto:
- If desired, drape thin slices of prosciutto over the salad for an added savory element.

Serve:
- Serve the peach and burrata salad immediately, allowing the flavors to meld.

This salad celebrates the simplicity and freshness of seasonal ingredients. The sweetness of the peaches pairs beautifully with the creamy burrata, and the combination of basil and mint adds a burst of herbaceous flavor. The drizzle of olive oil and balsamic glaze enhances the richness of the dish. Enjoy this peach and burrata salad as a light and elegant addition to your summer meals.

Zucchini Noodles with Pesto

Ingredients:

For the Zucchini Noodles:

- 4 medium-sized zucchini
- Salt for sprinkling

For the Pesto:

- 2 cups fresh basil leaves, packed
- 1/2 cup grated Parmesan cheese
- 1/2 cup pine nuts or walnuts
- 3 cloves garlic, peeled
- 1/2 cup extra-virgin olive oil
- Salt and black pepper to taste
- 1/2 cup grated Pecorino Romano cheese (optional)

Instructions:

Prepare the Zucchini Noodles:
- Use a spiralizer to create zucchini noodles. If you don't have a spiralizer, you can use a julienne peeler or a knife to cut the zucchini into thin strips.
- Sprinkle the zucchini noodles with salt and let them sit for about 15-20 minutes to release excess moisture.

Make the Pesto:
- In a food processor, combine the fresh basil, grated Parmesan cheese, pine nuts or walnuts, and peeled garlic cloves.
- Pulse the ingredients until coarsely chopped.
- With the food processor running, slowly pour in the olive oil until the pesto reaches a smooth consistency.
- Season with salt and black pepper to taste. Add more olive oil if needed.
- If using, mix in the grated Pecorino Romano cheese.

Drain Zucchini Noodles:

- After the zucchini noodles have released some moisture, use a clean kitchen towel or paper towels to pat them dry or gently squeeze out excess water.

Combine Zucchini Noodles and Pesto:
- In a large mixing bowl, toss the zucchini noodles with the homemade pesto until well coated.

Serve:
- Plate the zucchini noodles with pesto on serving dishes.

Optional Garnish:
- Optionally, garnish with additional grated Parmesan cheese or pine nuts.

Enjoy:
- Serve immediately and enjoy your light and flavorful zucchini noodles with pesto.

This zucchini noodle dish is not only delicious but also a great way to incorporate more vegetables into your meals. The homemade pesto adds a burst of fresh basil and nutty flavors, creating a vibrant and satisfying dish. Feel free to customize the pesto by adjusting the ingredient quantities based on your taste preferences.

California Veggie Burger

Ingredients:

For the Veggie Patties:

- 1 can (15 oz) black beans, drained and rinsed
- 1 cup cooked quinoa or brown rice
- 1 cup finely chopped mushrooms
- 1/2 cup grated carrot
- 1/4 cup finely chopped red onion
- 2 cloves garlic, minced
- 1 teaspoon ground cumin
- 1 teaspoon smoked paprika
- Salt and pepper to taste
- 1 tablespoon soy sauce or tamari
- 1 tablespoon olive oil for cooking

For Assembling the Burger:

- Whole grain burger buns
- Avocado slices
- Tomato slices
- Red onion rings
- Lettuce leaves
- Dijon mustard or your favorite sauce

Instructions:

Prepare the Veggie Patties:
- In a large bowl, mash the black beans with a fork or potato masher, leaving some chunks for texture.
- Add cooked quinoa or brown rice, chopped mushrooms, grated carrot, red onion, minced garlic, ground cumin, smoked paprika, salt, pepper, and soy sauce. Mix well until everything is combined.
- Form the mixture into patties. If the mixture is too wet, you can add a bit of breadcrumbs to help bind it.

Cook the Veggie Patties:
- Heat olive oil in a skillet over medium heat.

- Cook the veggie patties for 4-5 minutes on each side or until golden brown and cooked through.

Assemble the Burger:
- Toast the whole grain burger buns if desired.
- Spread Dijon mustard or your favorite sauce on the bottom half of the bun.
- Place a veggie patty on the bun.
- Top with avocado slices, tomato slices, red onion rings, and lettuce leaves.
- Cover with the other half of the bun.

Serve:
- Serve your California veggie burger with your favorite side dishes and enjoy!

Feel free to customize your California veggie burger with additional toppings like sprouts, pickles, or a special sauce. This recipe is versatile, and you can experiment with various herbs and spices to suit your taste preferences.

Lemon Herb Grilled Swordfish

Ingredients:

- 4 swordfish steaks (about 6-8 ounces each)
- Zest and juice of 1 lemon
- 2 tablespoons fresh chopped parsley
- 1 tablespoon fresh chopped thyme
- 2 cloves garlic, minced
- 1/4 cup extra-virgin olive oil
- Salt and black pepper to taste
- Lemon wedges for serving

Instructions:

Prepare the Marinade:
- In a bowl, whisk together the lemon zest, lemon juice, chopped parsley, chopped thyme, minced garlic, and olive oil. Season with salt and black pepper to taste.

Marinate the Swordfish:
- Place the swordfish steaks in a shallow dish or a zip-top bag. Pour the marinade over the swordfish, ensuring each piece is well-coated. Marinate in the refrigerator for at least 30 minutes, allowing the flavors to infuse.

Preheat the Grill:
- Preheat your grill to medium-high heat.

Grill the Swordfish:
- Remove the swordfish from the marinade and let any excess drip off.
- Grill the swordfish steaks for about 4-5 minutes per side, or until they are opaque and easily flake with a fork.

Baste with Marinade (Optional):
- Optionally, you can baste the swordfish with some of the marinade while grilling for added flavor.

Serve:
- Transfer the grilled swordfish steaks to a serving platter.
- Drizzle any remaining marinade over the top.
- Serve with lemon wedges on the side for squeezing over the fish.

Garnish (Optional):
- Garnish with additional fresh herbs for a burst of color and flavor.

Enjoy your lemon herb grilled swordfish as a main course, paired with your favorite side dishes such as a fresh salad or grilled vegetables. The combination of lemon and herbs adds brightness to the dish, enhancing the natural flavors of the swordfish.

Sweet Potato and Black Bean Enchiladas

Ingredients:

For the Filling:

- 2 medium-sized sweet potatoes, peeled and diced
- 1 can (15 oz) black beans, drained and rinsed
- 1 cup corn kernels (fresh, frozen, or canned)
- 1 red bell pepper, diced
- 1 small red onion, diced
- 2 cloves garlic, minced
- 1 teaspoon ground cumin
- 1 teaspoon chili powder
- Salt and black pepper to taste
- 2 tablespoons olive oil

For the Enchilada Sauce:

- 2 cups tomato sauce
- 1 teaspoon ground cumin
- 1 teaspoon chili powder
- 1/2 teaspoon garlic powder
- Salt to taste

Other Ingredients:

- 8 small flour or corn tortillas
- 2 cups shredded Mexican blend cheese
- Fresh cilantro, chopped, for garnish
- Lime wedges for serving

Instructions:

    Preheat the Oven:
- Preheat your oven to 375°F (190°C).

    Roast Sweet Potatoes:
- Toss the diced sweet potatoes with 1 tablespoon of olive oil, ground cumin, chili powder, salt, and black pepper.

- Spread them on a baking sheet and roast in the preheated oven for about 20-25 minutes or until the sweet potatoes are tender.

Prepare the Filling:
- In a skillet, heat the remaining 1 tablespoon of olive oil. Add diced red bell pepper, red onion, and minced garlic. Sauté until softened.
- Add the roasted sweet potatoes, black beans, and corn to the skillet. Stir in ground cumin, chili powder, salt, and black pepper. Cook for an additional 2-3 minutes until the filling is well combined and heated through.

Make the Enchilada Sauce:
- In a separate bowl, whisk together tomato sauce, ground cumin, chili powder, garlic powder, and salt. This will be your enchilada sauce.

Assemble the Enchiladas:
- Spread a small amount of enchilada sauce on the bottom of a baking dish.
- Spoon the sweet potato and black bean filling into each tortilla, roll them up, and place them seam-side down in the baking dish.

Pour Sauce and Add Cheese:
- Pour the remaining enchilada sauce over the rolled tortillas.
- Sprinkle shredded cheese on top.

Bake:
- Bake in the preheated oven for 20-25 minutes or until the cheese is melted and bubbly.

Garnish and Serve:
- Garnish with chopped cilantro and serve with lime wedges.

These sweet potato and black bean enchiladas are a flavorful and wholesome dish, perfect for a satisfying vegetarian meal. Serve them with your favorite toppings such as sour cream, avocado slices, or salsa for an extra burst of flavor.

Mexican Street Corn Salad

Ingredients:

- 4 cups cooked corn kernels (fresh, frozen, or canned)
- 1/2 cup mayonnaise
- 1/4 cup sour cream
- 1/2 cup crumbled feta cheese or cotija cheese
- 1/4 cup finely chopped fresh cilantro
- 2 tablespoons finely chopped green onions
- 1 teaspoon chili powder (adjust to taste)
- 1 clove garlic, minced
- Juice of 1 lime
- Salt and black pepper to taste
- Optional: Hot sauce (e.g., Tajín or Tapatio) for extra heat
- Lime wedges for serving

Instructions:

Cook Corn:
- If using fresh corn, boil or grill the corn until it's cooked. If using frozen or canned corn, follow the package instructions.

Prepare Dressing:
- In a large bowl, whisk together mayonnaise, sour cream, minced garlic, lime juice, chili powder, salt, and black pepper.

Combine Ingredients:
- Add the cooked corn to the bowl with the dressing.
- Mix well to coat the corn with the dressing.

Add Cheese and Herbs:
- Fold in the crumbled feta or cotija cheese, chopped cilantro, and green onions. Mix until evenly distributed.

Adjust Seasonings:
- Taste the salad and adjust the seasoning, adding more salt, pepper, or chili powder if needed. If you like it spicy, you can also add hot sauce to your liking.

Chill (Optional):
- Refrigerate the salad for at least 30 minutes to allow the flavors to meld.

Serve:

- Serve the Mexican street corn salad in individual bowls or cups.
- Optionally, sprinkle additional chili powder or crumbled cheese on top.

Garnish and Enjoy:
- Garnish with lime wedges and serve. Enjoy your delicious Mexican street corn salad!

This vibrant and flavorful salad is a great side dish for barbecues, picnics, or as a refreshing addition to your Mexican-inspired meals. Adjust the ingredients and spice levels according to your preferences for a perfect balance of creaminess, tanginess, and smoky chili flavors.

California Caprese Skewers

Ingredients:

- Cherry tomatoes
- Fresh mozzarella balls (bocconcini)
- Avocado, cut into bite-sized cubes
- Fresh basil leaves
- Balsamic glaze for drizzling
- Olive oil for drizzling
- Salt and black pepper to taste
- Optional: Wooden skewers for assembling

Instructions:

Prepare Ingredients:
- Wash and dry the cherry tomatoes.
- Drain the fresh mozzarella balls.
- Cut the avocado into bite-sized cubes.
- Pick fresh basil leaves from the stems.

Assemble the Skewers:
- If using wooden skewers, thread a cherry tomato, followed by a mozzarella ball, a basil leaf, and a cube of avocado onto each skewer.
- Repeat the process until you have assembled all the skewers.

Arrange on a Platter:
- Arrange the California Caprese skewers on a serving platter.

Drizzle with Olive Oil:
- Drizzle olive oil over the skewers.

Season:
- Sprinkle salt and black pepper to taste.

Drizzle with Balsamic Glaze:
- Drizzle balsamic glaze over the skewers for a sweet and tangy finish.

Serve:
- Serve the California Caprese skewers immediately.

These skewers are a delightful appetizer or snack, showcasing the fresh and vibrant flavors of California produce. The combination of juicy cherry tomatoes, creamy mozzarella, buttery avocado, and fragrant basil creates a perfect harmony of taste and textures. The drizzle of olive oil and balsamic glaze adds a finishing touch that enhances the overall flavor profile. Enjoy these California Caprese skewers as a refreshing and visually appealing dish for any occasion.

Lemon Thyme Roasted Chicken

Ingredients:

- 1 whole chicken (about 4-5 pounds)
- Salt and black pepper to taste
- 2 tablespoons fresh thyme leaves
- Zest of 1 lemon
- 2 tablespoons olive oil
- 4 cloves garlic, minced
- Juice of 1 lemon
- 1 cup chicken broth or water
- 1 onion, quartered
- 2 lemons, sliced
- Fresh thyme sprigs for garnish (optional)

Instructions:

Preheat the Oven:
- Preheat your oven to 425°F (220°C).

Prepare the Chicken:
- Rinse the chicken under cold water and pat it dry with paper towels.
- Season the chicken cavity with salt and pepper.

Season the Chicken Skin:
- In a small bowl, mix together the fresh thyme leaves, lemon zest, olive oil, and minced garlic.
- Rub the thyme and lemon mixture all over the chicken, ensuring it's evenly coated. Season the skin with salt and black pepper.

Stuffed with Aromatics:
- Stuff the chicken cavity with lemon slices, onion quarters, and a few sprigs of fresh thyme.

Truss the Chicken (Optional):
- Truss the chicken with kitchen twine to help it cook evenly.

Place in Roasting Pan:
- Place the prepared chicken in a roasting pan, breast side up.

Squeeze Lemon Juice:
- Squeeze the juice of one lemon over the top of the chicken.

Add Liquid:
- Pour chicken broth or water into the bottom of the roasting pan.

Roast in the Oven:
- Roast the chicken in the preheated oven for about 1 hour and 15 minutes to 1 hour and 30 minutes, or until the internal temperature reaches 165°F (74°C).

Baste the Chicken:
- Baste the chicken with pan juices every 30 minutes to keep it moist.

Rest Before Carving:
- Once the chicken is done, let it rest for about 10-15 minutes before carving.

Garnish and Serve:
- Garnish with fresh thyme sprigs if desired and serve.

This lemon thyme roasted chicken is succulent, aromatic, and perfect for a family dinner or special occasion. The combination of citrusy lemon, fragrant thyme, and garlic infuses the chicken with delightful flavors. Serve it with your favorite side dishes for a complete and satisfying meal.

Teriyaki Tofu Stir-Fry

Ingredients:

For the Tofu:

- 1 block extra-firm tofu, pressed and cubed
- 2 tablespoons soy sauce
- 1 tablespoon cornstarch
- 1 tablespoon sesame oil
- 1 tablespoon vegetable oil for cooking

For the Stir-Fry:

- 1 tablespoon vegetable oil
- 1 bell pepper, thinly sliced
- 1 carrot, julienned
- 1 broccoli crown, cut into florets
- 1 cup snap peas, ends trimmed
- 2 cloves garlic, minced
- 1 tablespoon fresh ginger, minced

For the Teriyaki Sauce:

- 1/4 cup soy sauce
- 2 tablespoons mirin
- 2 tablespoons sake (or rice vinegar)
- 2 tablespoons brown sugar
- 1 tablespoon cornstarch mixed with 2 tablespoons water (cornstarch slurry)

To Serve:

- Cooked brown or white rice
- Sesame seeds for garnish (optional)
- Green onions, sliced for garnish (optional)

Instructions:

   Prepare the Tofu:

- Press the tofu to remove excess water by wrapping it in paper towels and placing something heavy on top for about 30 minutes. Cut the pressed tofu into cubes.
- In a bowl, toss the tofu cubes with soy sauce, cornstarch, and sesame oil.

Cook the Tofu:
- Heat vegetable oil in a large skillet or wok over medium-high heat.
- Add the tofu cubes and cook until all sides are golden and crisp. Remove tofu from the pan and set aside.

Prepare the Teriyaki Sauce:
- In a small bowl, whisk together soy sauce, mirin, sake (or rice vinegar), brown sugar, and cornstarch slurry.

Stir-Fry Vegetables:
- In the same skillet or wok, add another tablespoon of vegetable oil.
- Stir-fry bell pepper, carrot, broccoli, snap peas, minced garlic, and minced ginger until the vegetables are tender-crisp.

Combine Tofu and Sauce:
- Add the cooked tofu back to the pan with the vegetables.
- Pour the teriyaki sauce over the tofu and vegetables. Stir well to coat everything evenly.

Simmer and Thicken:
- Allow the sauce to simmer for a few minutes until it thickens and coats the tofu and vegetables.

Serve:
- Serve the teriyaki tofu stir-fry over cooked rice.
- Garnish with sesame seeds and sliced green onions if desired.

This teriyaki tofu stir-fry is a delicious and wholesome vegetarian option that's packed with protein and vibrant vegetables. Adjust the sweetness and saltiness of the teriyaki sauce according to your taste preferences. Enjoy this flavorful dish as a quick and easy weeknight meal.

California Rice Bowl

Ingredients:

For the Rice Bowl Base:

- 2 cups cooked brown rice or quinoa

For the Protein (Choose One or Mix):

- Grilled chicken strips
- Tofu cubes (marinated and sautéed)
- Shrimp (grilled or sautéed)
- Black beans (canned, drained, and rinsed)

For the Vegetables (Mix and Match):

- Avocado slices
- Cherry tomatoes, halved
- Cucumber slices
- Shredded carrots
- Mixed greens or spinach
- Bell pepper strips
- Red onion, thinly sliced
- Corn kernels (fresh, frozen, or canned)

For the Dressing:

- 3 tablespoons olive oil
- 2 tablespoons balsamic vinegar or rice vinegar
- 1 tablespoon Dijon mustard
- Salt and black pepper to taste

Optional Toppings:

- Sliced almonds
- Feta or goat cheese crumbles
- Fresh herbs (cilantro, parsley, or basil)

Instructions:

Prepare the Rice or Quinoa:
- Cook brown rice or quinoa according to package instructions.

Prepare the Protein:
- Cook your choice of protein (grilled chicken, tofu, shrimp, or black beans) with your preferred seasoning.

Chop Vegetables:
- Wash and chop the vegetables you want to include in your bowl.

Make the Dressing:
- In a small bowl, whisk together olive oil, balsamic vinegar, Dijon mustard, salt, and black pepper to create the dressing.

Assemble the Rice Bowl:
- In each bowl, start with a base of cooked rice or quinoa.
- Arrange your chosen protein and vegetables on top of the rice.

Drizzle with Dressing:
- Drizzle the dressing over the rice and vegetables.

Add Optional Toppings:
- Sprinkle sliced almonds, feta or goat cheese crumbles, and fresh herbs for extra flavor.

Mix and Enjoy:
- Toss the ingredients gently to combine or leave them layered for a visually appealing presentation.
- Enjoy your California rice bowl!

This California rice bowl is not only delicious but also a nutritious and balanced meal. Feel free to get creative with your choice of ingredients, and adjust the dressing to suit your taste preferences. It's a perfect dish for a quick and healthy lunch or dinner.

Grilled Portobello Mushrooms with Pesto

Ingredients:

For the Grilled Portobello Mushrooms:

- 4 large portobello mushrooms, stems removed
- 2 tablespoons balsamic vinegar
- 2 tablespoons olive oil
- 2 cloves garlic, minced
- Salt and black pepper to taste

For the Pesto:

- 2 cups fresh basil leaves, packed
- 1/2 cup grated Parmesan cheese
- 1/2 cup pine nuts or walnuts
- 2 cloves garlic, peeled
- 1/2 cup extra-virgin olive oil
- Salt and black pepper to taste

Instructions:

Marinate the Mushrooms:
- In a bowl, whisk together balsamic vinegar, olive oil, minced garlic, salt, and black pepper.
- Place the portobello mushrooms in a shallow dish and brush both sides with the marinade. Let them marinate for about 15-30 minutes.

Prepare the Pesto:
- In a food processor, combine fresh basil, grated Parmesan cheese, pine nuts or walnuts, and peeled garlic cloves.
- Pulse the ingredients until coarsely chopped.
- With the food processor running, slowly pour in the olive oil until the pesto reaches a smooth consistency.
- Season with salt and black pepper to taste.

Preheat the Grill:
- Preheat your grill or grill pan to medium-high heat.

Grill the Portobello Mushrooms:
- Place the marinated portobello mushrooms on the preheated grill.

- Grill for about 4-5 minutes per side or until the mushrooms are tender and have grill marks.

Assemble with Pesto:
- Once the mushrooms are grilled, spread a generous amount of pesto over the gill side of each mushroom.

Serve:
- Serve the grilled portobello mushrooms with pesto immediately.

This dish highlights the earthy flavor of portobello mushrooms complemented by the fresh and herby notes of the pesto. It's a delicious and elegant option for a vegetarian meal or a flavorful side dish. Enjoy it on its own or serve it alongside a salad or your favorite grains for a complete and satisfying meal.

Citrus-Marinated Grilled Lamb Chops

Ingredients:

For the Marinade:

- 1/4 cup olive oil
- 2 tablespoons fresh lemon juice
- 2 tablespoons fresh orange juice
- 1 tablespoon Dijon mustard
- 2 cloves garlic, minced
- 1 teaspoon dried oregano
- 1 teaspoon dried rosemary
- Salt and black pepper to taste

For the Lamb Chops:

- 8 lamb chops, about 1 inch thick
- Salt and black pepper to taste

For Garnish (optional):

- Fresh herbs (parsley, mint, or cilantro), chopped
- Lemon or orange wedges

Instructions:

Prepare the Marinade:
- In a bowl, whisk together olive oil, fresh lemon juice, fresh orange juice, Dijon mustard, minced garlic, dried oregano, dried rosemary, salt, and black pepper.

Marinate the Lamb Chops:
- Place the lamb chops in a shallow dish or a resealable plastic bag.
- Pour the marinade over the lamb chops, ensuring they are well-coated.
- Marinate in the refrigerator for at least 2 hours, or preferably overnight for more flavor.

Preheat the Grill:

- Preheat your grill to medium-high heat.

Season the Lamb Chops:
- Remove the lamb chops from the marinade and let excess marinade drip off.
- Season the lamb chops with additional salt and black pepper to taste.

Grill the Lamb Chops:
- Grill the lamb chops for about 3-4 minutes per side for medium-rare, or adjust the cooking time to your preferred doneness.

Rest and Garnish:
- Let the grilled lamb chops rest for a few minutes before serving.
- Optionally, garnish with fresh chopped herbs and serve with lemon or orange wedges on the side.

Serve:
- Plate the grilled lamb chops and serve immediately.

These citrus-marinated grilled lamb chops are a delightful combination of savory and zesty flavors. The marinade infuses the lamb with a refreshing citrus kick, while the grilling process adds a beautiful char and smokiness. Serve these lamb chops with your favorite sides, such as roasted vegetables, couscous, or a fresh salad, for a complete and delicious meal.

Mediterranean Quinoa Salad

Ingredients:

For the Salad:

- 1 cup quinoa, rinsed and cooked according to package instructions
- 1 cucumber, diced
- 1 cup cherry tomatoes, halved
- 1/2 cup Kalamata olives, pitted and sliced
- 1/2 cup red onion, finely chopped
- 1/2 cup feta cheese, crumbled
- 1/4 cup fresh parsley, chopped
- 1/4 cup fresh mint, chopped (optional)
- Salt and black pepper to taste

For the Dressing:

- 1/4 cup extra-virgin olive oil
- 2 tablespoons red wine vinegar
- 1 clove garlic, minced
- 1 teaspoon dried oregano
- Salt and black pepper to taste

Instructions:

Cook Quinoa:
- Rinse quinoa under cold water. Cook quinoa according to package instructions. Once cooked, fluff it with a fork and let it cool to room temperature.

Prepare Vegetables:
- Dice the cucumber, halve the cherry tomatoes, slice the Kalamata olives, finely chop the red onion, and crumble the feta cheese.

Make the Dressing:
- In a small bowl, whisk together olive oil, red wine vinegar, minced garlic, dried oregano, salt, and black pepper to create the dressing.

Assemble the Salad:

- In a large mixing bowl, combine the cooked quinoa, diced cucumber, halved cherry tomatoes, sliced Kalamata olives, chopped red onion, crumbled feta cheese, fresh parsley, and optional fresh mint.

Drizzle with Dressing:
- Pour the dressing over the salad ingredients.

Toss and Season:
- Gently toss the salad to coat the ingredients evenly with the dressing.
- Season with additional salt and black pepper to taste.

Chill (Optional):
- For enhanced flavors, refrigerate the salad for at least 30 minutes before serving.

Serve:
- Serve the Mediterranean quinoa salad on its own or as a side dish.

This Mediterranean quinoa salad is a wonderful combination of textures and flavors, from the fluffy quinoa to the crisp vegetables and the tangy feta cheese. The dressing with olive oil, red wine vinegar, and herbs ties everything together for a light and refreshing dish. Enjoy it as a healthy lunch, a side dish, or bring it to picnics and potlucks for a crowd-pleasing option.

Spicy Sriracha Shrimp Lettuce Wraps

Ingredients:

For the Sriracha Shrimp:

- 1 pound large shrimp, peeled and deveined
- 2 tablespoons soy sauce
- 1 tablespoon Sriracha sauce (adjust to taste)
- 1 tablespoon honey or maple syrup
- 1 tablespoon sesame oil
- 2 cloves garlic, minced
- 1 teaspoon grated ginger
- 1 tablespoon olive oil for cooking

For the Lettuce Wraps:

- Large lettuce leaves (such as iceberg or butter lettuce)
- Thinly sliced cucumber
- Matchstick carrots
- Sliced red bell pepper
- Fresh cilantro leaves
- Lime wedges for serving

Instructions:

Prepare the Sriracha Shrimp:
- In a bowl, whisk together soy sauce, Sriracha sauce, honey or maple syrup, sesame oil, minced garlic, and grated ginger.
- Add the peeled and deveined shrimp to the marinade, tossing to coat. Let it marinate for about 15-20 minutes.

Cook the Sriracha Shrimp:
- Heat olive oil in a skillet over medium-high heat.
- Add the marinated shrimp to the skillet and cook for 2-3 minutes per side or until the shrimp are pink and opaque. Be careful not to overcook.

Prepare Lettuce Wraps:
- Wash and separate large lettuce leaves to create cups for the wraps.

- Fill each lettuce cup with Sriracha shrimp.

Add Vegetables:
- Top the shrimp with thinly sliced cucumber, matchstick carrots, sliced red bell pepper, and fresh cilantro leaves.

Serve:
- Squeeze lime wedges over the top and serve the spicy Sriracha shrimp lettuce wraps immediately.

These lettuce wraps are not only delicious but also customizable. You can add other fresh vegetables or toppings like avocado, bean sprouts, or chopped peanuts for additional texture and flavor. Enjoy these spicy Sriracha shrimp lettuce wraps as a light and satisfying meal.

California Fig and Goat Cheese Pizza

Ingredients:

- 1 pizza dough (store-bought or homemade)
- Olive oil for brushing
- 1 cup crumbled goat cheese
- 1 cup fresh figs, sliced
- 1/4 cup honey
- 1/4 cup balsamic reduction (balsamic glaze)
- Fresh arugula for topping
- Salt and black pepper to taste

Instructions:

Preheat the Oven:
- Preheat your oven to the temperature recommended for your pizza dough.

Roll Out the Pizza Dough:
- Roll out the pizza dough on a floured surface to your desired thickness.

Prepare the Pizza:
- Transfer the rolled-out dough to a pizza stone or a baking sheet.
- Brush the surface of the dough with olive oil.

Add Goat Cheese and Figs:
- Sprinkle crumbled goat cheese evenly over the pizza dough.
- Arrange the sliced fresh figs on top of the goat cheese.

Bake the Pizza:
- Bake in the preheated oven according to the pizza dough instructions, typically around 12-15 minutes or until the crust is golden and the cheese is melted.

Drizzle with Honey and Balsamic Reduction:
- Once the pizza is out of the oven, drizzle honey and balsamic reduction over the top.

Add Fresh Arugula:
- Scatter fresh arugula over the pizza for a peppery bite.

Season and Serve:
- Season the pizza with a pinch of salt and black pepper.
- Slice and serve immediately.

This California Fig and Goat Cheese Pizza is a perfect blend of sweet and savory, making it a delicious option for a light lunch or dinner. The creamy goat cheese, sweet figs, and the drizzle of honey create a harmonious flavor profile, while the arugula adds a fresh and vibrant touch. Enjoy this pizza as a unique and gourmet twist on the traditional.

Cilantro Lime Grilled Corn

Ingredients:

- 4 ears of corn, husked
- 2 tablespoons unsalted butter, melted
- Zest and juice of 1 lime
- 1/4 cup fresh cilantro, chopped
- Salt and black pepper to taste
- Grated cotija cheese (optional, for garnish)

Instructions:

Preheat the Grill:
- Preheat your grill to medium-high heat.

Prepare the Corn:
- Husk the corn, removing the silk, and brush each ear with melted butter.

Grill the Corn:
- Place the corn directly on the preheated grill.

Rotate and Cook:
- Rotate the corn occasionally to ensure even grilling.
- Grill for about 10-12 minutes or until the corn is tender and has a nice char.

Prepare the Cilantro Lime Mixture:
- While the corn is grilling, mix the lime zest, lime juice, and chopped cilantro in a small bowl.

Brush with Cilantro Lime Mixture:
- Once the corn is done, brush each ear with the cilantro lime mixture.

Season and Garnish:
- Sprinkle salt and black pepper to taste.
- Optionally, garnish with grated cotija cheese for an extra burst of flavor.

Serve:
- Serve the cilantro lime grilled corn immediately.

Enjoy this cilantro lime grilled corn as a flavorful and vibrant side dish at your next barbecue or summer gathering. The combination of the smoky grilled corn, zesty lime, and fresh cilantro creates a delicious and refreshing flavor profile that's sure to be a hit.

Tomato Basil Bruschetta

Ingredients:

- 4-5 ripe tomatoes, diced
- 1/2 cup fresh basil leaves, chopped
- 2-3 cloves garlic, minced
- 1/4 cup extra-virgin olive oil
- 1 teaspoon balsamic vinegar
- Salt and black pepper to taste
- Baguette or Italian bread, sliced

Instructions:

Prepare the Tomatoes:
- Dice the ripe tomatoes and place them in a large bowl.

Chop the Basil:
- Chop the fresh basil leaves finely and add them to the bowl with the tomatoes.

Add Garlic:
- Mince the garlic cloves and add them to the bowl.

Drizzle with Olive Oil:
- Drizzle extra-virgin olive oil over the tomato, basil, and garlic mixture.

Splash of Balsamic Vinegar:
- Add a teaspoon of balsamic vinegar for a hint of sweetness and acidity.

Season:
- Season the mixture with salt and black pepper to taste.

Mix Well:
- Gently toss all the ingredients together until well combined. Be careful not to mash the tomatoes.

Let it Marinate:
- Allow the mixture to marinate for at least 15-30 minutes to let the flavors meld.

Toast the Bread:
- While the tomato mixture is marinating, slice the baguette or Italian bread.
- Toast the bread slices in a toaster or on a grill until they are golden and crisp.

Assemble and Serve:

- Spoon the tomato basil mixture onto the toasted bread slices.
- Arrange the bruschetta on a serving platter.

Optional Garnish:
- Optionally, garnish with additional fresh basil leaves for a pop of color.

Serve Immediately:
- Serve the tomato basil bruschetta immediately.

This classic tomato basil bruschetta is a perfect appetizer for any occasion. The combination of ripe tomatoes, fragrant basil, and garlic creates a delightful topping for the crunchy and toasted bread. It's a crowd-pleaser and a great way to showcase the flavors of fresh summer tomatoes. Enjoy!

Pomegranate Glazed Salmon

Ingredients:

For the Pomegranate Glaze:

- 1 cup pomegranate juice (freshly squeezed or store-bought)
- 1/4 cup honey
- 2 tablespoons soy sauce
- 1 tablespoon Dijon mustard
- 1 clove garlic, minced
- Salt and black pepper to taste

For the Salmon:

- 4 salmon fillets
- Salt and black pepper to taste
- 1 tablespoon olive oil
- Fresh pomegranate arils (seeds) for garnish (optional)
- Chopped fresh parsley for garnish (optional)

Instructions:

Prepare the Pomegranate Glaze:
- In a small saucepan, combine pomegranate juice, honey, soy sauce, Dijon mustard, minced garlic, salt, and black pepper.
- Bring the mixture to a simmer over medium heat and let it cook for about 10-15 minutes or until the glaze thickens slightly.

Season the Salmon:
- Season the salmon fillets with salt and black pepper.

Preheat the Oven:
- Preheat your oven to 400°F (200°C).

Sear the Salmon:
- In an oven-safe skillet, heat olive oil over medium-high heat.
- Sear the salmon fillets, skin side down, for 2-3 minutes until the skin is crispy.

Apply Pomegranate Glaze:

- Brush the top of each salmon fillet with the prepared pomegranate glaze.

Bake in the Oven:
- Transfer the skillet to the preheated oven and bake for 10-12 minutes or until the salmon is cooked to your liking.

Glaze Again:
- Brush an additional layer of pomegranate glaze over the salmon during the last few minutes of baking.

Garnish and Serve:
- Once the salmon is cooked through, remove it from the oven.
- Garnish with fresh pomegranate arils and chopped parsley if desired.

Serve Warm:
- Serve the pomegranate glazed salmon warm.

This pomegranate glazed salmon is a perfect dish for special occasions or a fancy dinner at home. The glaze adds a beautiful sheen and a burst of sweet and tart flavor to the rich salmon. Enjoy it with your favorite side dishes, such as roasted vegetables or quinoa, for a complete and delicious meal.

California-Style Turkey Club

Ingredients:

- 8 slices of your favorite bread (sourdough, whole wheat, or multigrain)
- 1/2 cup mayonnaise
- 1 tablespoon Dijon mustard
- 1 pound roasted turkey breast, sliced
- 8 slices bacon, cooked until crispy
- 1 large avocado, sliced
- 1 large tomato, sliced
- 1 cup fresh lettuce or spinach leaves
- Salt and black pepper to taste

Instructions:

Prepare the Spread:
- In a small bowl, mix mayonnaise and Dijon mustard to create a flavorful spread.

Toast the Bread:
- Toast the slices of bread to your liking.

Assemble the Sandwiches:
- Spread the mayo-Dijon mixture on one side of each slice of bread.

Layer the Ingredients:
- On four slices of bread, layer the roasted turkey slices, crispy bacon, avocado slices, tomato slices, and fresh lettuce or spinach leaves.

Season:
- Season the layers with salt and black pepper to taste.

Top and Close:
- Place the remaining slices of bread on top, mayo-side down, to create four sandwiches.

Cut and Serve:
- Use a sharp knife to cut each sandwich diagonally into halves or quarters.

Serve:
- Serve the California-style turkey club sandwiches immediately.

These California-style turkey club sandwiches showcase the freshness and flavors of the region. The combination of juicy turkey, crispy bacon, creamy avocado, ripe tomatoes, and crisp lettuce makes for a satisfying and tasty meal. Enjoy this sandwich for lunch, dinner, or as a delightful addition to your picnic or casual gathering.

Herb-Roasted Baby Potatoes

Ingredients:

- 1.5 pounds baby potatoes, washed and halved
- 2 tablespoons olive oil
- 2 cloves garlic, minced
- 1 teaspoon dried rosemary
- 1 teaspoon dried thyme
- 1 teaspoon dried oregano
- Salt and black pepper to taste
- Fresh parsley, chopped (for garnish, optional)

Instructions:

Preheat the Oven:
- Preheat your oven to 400°F (200°C).

Prepare the Potatoes:
- Wash the baby potatoes thoroughly and cut them in half. If they are slightly larger, you can quarter them.

Herb Mixture:
- In a large bowl, combine olive oil, minced garlic, dried rosemary, dried thyme, dried oregano, salt, and black pepper.

Coat the Potatoes:
- Add the halved baby potatoes to the bowl with the herb mixture. Toss until the potatoes are evenly coated.

Roasting Pan:
- Transfer the coated potatoes to a roasting pan or baking sheet, spreading them out in a single layer.

Roast in the Oven:
- Roast the potatoes in the preheated oven for about 25-30 minutes or until they are golden brown and crispy on the edges. Toss them once halfway through the cooking time for even roasting.

Check for Doneness:
- Pierce a potato with a fork to check for doneness; it should be tender on the inside.

Garnish and Serve:
- Once the potatoes are done, remove them from the oven.
- Garnish with chopped fresh parsley if desired.

Serve Warm:
- Serve the herb-roasted baby potatoes warm as a delicious side dish.

These herb-roasted baby potatoes are a versatile and tasty side that pairs well with various proteins or can be enjoyed on their own. The combination of olive oil and herbs gives the potatoes a flavorful and aromatic crust. They are perfect for weeknight dinners, holiday meals, or any gathering where you want a simple and delicious side dish.

Spinach and Feta Stuffed Chicken Breast

Ingredients:

- 4 boneless, skinless chicken breasts
- Salt and black pepper to taste
- 2 cups fresh spinach, chopped
- 1/2 cup crumbled feta cheese
- 2 tablespoons olive oil
- 2 cloves garlic, minced
- 1 teaspoon dried oregano
- 1 teaspoon dried thyme
- 1 teaspoon paprika
- Toothpicks or kitchen twine

Instructions:

Preheat the Oven:
- Preheat your oven to 375°F (190°C).

Prepare the Chicken:
- Lay each chicken breast flat on a cutting board. Using a sharp knife, make a horizontal cut into the thickest side of the breast, creating a pocket without cutting all the way through.

Season the Chicken:
- Season the inside and outside of each chicken breast with salt and black pepper.

Make the Filling:
- In a bowl, combine chopped spinach, crumbled feta cheese, minced garlic, dried oregano, dried thyme, and paprika.

Stuff the Chicken:
- Stuff each chicken breast with the spinach and feta mixture, pressing down gently to pack the filling.

Secure with Toothpicks or Kitchen Twine:
- Use toothpicks or kitchen twine to secure the opening of each stuffed chicken breast, ensuring the filling stays inside during cooking.

Sear the Chicken:
- Heat olive oil in an oven-safe skillet over medium-high heat. Sear the stuffed chicken breasts for 2-3 minutes on each side until they develop a golden-brown crust.

Finish in the Oven:
- Transfer the skillet to the preheated oven and bake for about 20-25 minutes or until the internal temperature of the chicken reaches 165°F (74°C).

Rest and Serve:
- Let the stuffed chicken breasts rest for a few minutes before removing toothpicks or twine.
- Slice and serve warm.

This spinach and feta stuffed chicken breast is a delicious and elegant dish that's perfect for a special dinner. The combination of the savory chicken, creamy feta, and vibrant spinach creates a delightful flavor profile. Serve it alongside your favorite sides, such as roasted vegetables or a light salad, for a complete and satisfying meal.

California Sunrise Smoothie

Ingredients:

- 1 cup fresh orange juice
- 1/2 cup pineapple chunks (fresh or frozen)
- 1/2 cup mango chunks (fresh or frozen)
- 1/2 cup strawberries (fresh or frozen)
- 1 banana
- 1/2 cup Greek yogurt or non-dairy yogurt for a vegan option
- Ice cubes (optional)
- Honey or agave syrup for sweetness (optional)

Instructions:

Prepare the Fruits:
- If you haven't already, peel and chop the banana. For pineapple, mango, and strawberries, ensure they are cleaned, peeled, and cut into chunks.

Combine Ingredients:
- In a blender, add the fresh orange juice, pineapple chunks, mango chunks, strawberries, banana, and Greek yogurt.

Optional Sweetener:
- If you prefer a sweeter smoothie, add honey or agave syrup to taste.

Blend Until Smooth:
- Blend all the ingredients until smooth and creamy. If the consistency is too thick, you can add a few ice cubes and blend again.

Taste and Adjust:
- Taste the smoothie and adjust the sweetness or consistency according to your preference.

Serve:
- Pour the California Sunrise Smoothie into glasses.

Garnish (Optional):
- Garnish with a slice of orange or a strawberry on the rim of the glass for a decorative touch.

Enjoy:
- Enjoy your California Sunrise Smoothie immediately.

This smoothie is not only delicious but also packed with vitamins and antioxidants from the variety of fruits. It's a perfect way to start your day or enjoy a refreshing pick-me-up in the afternoon. Feel free to customize the ingredients based on your taste preferences or the fruits available to you.

Miso Glazed Eggplant

Ingredients:

- 2 large eggplants, sliced into rounds or lengthwise
- 3 tablespoons white miso paste
- 2 tablespoons soy sauce
- 2 tablespoons mirin (sweet rice wine)
- 1 tablespoon sake (Japanese rice wine) or dry white wine
- 1 tablespoon sesame oil
- 1 tablespoon honey or maple syrup
- 2 cloves garlic, minced
- 1 tablespoon grated fresh ginger
- Sesame seeds and chopped green onions for garnish

Instructions:

Preheat the Oven:
- Preheat your oven to 400°F (200°C).

Prepare the Miso Glaze:
- In a bowl, whisk together miso paste, soy sauce, mirin, sake, sesame oil, honey or maple syrup, minced garlic, and grated fresh ginger. Mix until well combined.

Slice the Eggplant:
- Slice the eggplants into rounds or lengthwise, depending on your preference.

Brush with Miso Glaze:
- Brush both sides of each eggplant slice generously with the miso glaze.

Roast in the Oven:
- Place the glazed eggplant slices on a baking sheet lined with parchment paper.
- Roast in the preheated oven for about 20-25 minutes or until the eggplant is tender and caramelized, flipping the slices halfway through the cooking time.

Garnish:
- Remove the miso glazed eggplant from the oven and garnish with sesame seeds and chopped green onions.

Serve:

- Serve the miso glazed eggplant warm as a side dish or as part of a larger meal.

This dish is a wonderful balance of sweet, savory, and umami flavors. The miso glaze adds depth to the roasted eggplant, making it a delicious and satisfying dish. Enjoy it as a side, serve it over rice, or incorporate it into a bowl with other vegetables and proteins for a flavorful meal.

Caprese Stuffed Avocado

Ingredients:

- 2 ripe avocados, halved and pitted
- 1 cup cherry tomatoes, halved
- 1 cup fresh mozzarella pearls or diced fresh mozzarella
- Fresh basil leaves, torn or chopped
- Balsamic glaze or balsamic reduction for drizzling
- Extra-virgin olive oil for drizzling
- Salt and black pepper to taste

Instructions:

Prepare the Avocados:
- Cut the avocados in half and remove the pits.

Scoop the Center:
- If necessary, scoop out a small portion of the avocado flesh from each half to create a larger well for the stuffing.

Assemble the Filling:
- In a bowl, combine cherry tomatoes, fresh mozzarella, and torn or chopped basil leaves.

Season the Filling:
- Season the mixture with salt and black pepper to taste.

Fill the Avocados:
- Spoon the Caprese filling into the well of each avocado half.

Drizzle with Balsamic Glaze and Olive Oil:
- Drizzle balsamic glaze or balsamic reduction over the stuffed avocados.
- Drizzle extra-virgin olive oil for added richness.

Serve:
- Serve the Caprese stuffed avocados immediately.

This dish is a delightful combination of creamy avocado, juicy tomatoes, fresh mozzarella, and aromatic basil. The balsamic glaze adds a sweet and tangy flavor that ties everything together. Enjoy the Caprese stuffed avocados as a light and flavorful appetizer or a refreshing side dish.

Chickpea and Roasted Red Pepper Hummus Wrap

Ingredients:

- 1 large whole-grain or spinach tortilla
- 1/2 cup chickpeas (canned or cooked), mashed
- 2 tablespoons roasted red pepper hummus
- 1/4 cup cucumber, thinly sliced
- 1/4 cup cherry tomatoes, halved
- 1/4 cup red onion, thinly sliced
- 1/4 cup feta cheese, crumbled
- Fresh lettuce or spinach leaves
- Salt and black pepper to taste

Instructions:

Prepare the Chickpeas:
- If using canned chickpeas, drain and rinse them. Mash the chickpeas with a fork or potato masher.

Assemble the Wrap:
- Lay the tortilla on a flat surface.
- Spread the roasted red pepper hummus evenly over the tortilla.

Layer Ingredients:
- Add a layer of mashed chickpeas over the hummus.
- Arrange cucumber slices, halved cherry tomatoes, thinly sliced red onion, crumbled feta cheese, and fresh lettuce or spinach leaves on top.

Season:
- Season with salt and black pepper to taste.

Fold and Roll:
- Carefully fold in the sides of the tortilla and then roll it up tightly from the bottom to create a wrap.

Serve:
- Slice the wrap in half diagonally, if desired, and serve.

This Chickpea and Roasted Red Pepper Hummus Wrap is not only delicious but also packed with protein, fiber, and various nutrients. It's a perfect option for a quick and nutritious lunch or dinner. Feel free to customize the ingredients based on your preferences, adding avocado, olives, or other veggies for additional flavors and textures.

Coconut Lime Shrimp Tacos

Ingredients:

For the Coconut Lime Shrimp:

- 1 pound large shrimp, peeled and deveined
- 1 cup unsweetened coconut milk
- Zest and juice of 2 limes
- 2 tablespoons soy sauce
- 2 tablespoons honey or maple syrup
- 2 cloves garlic, minced
- 1 teaspoon grated ginger
- Salt and black pepper to taste
- 2 tablespoons coconut oil for cooking

For the Tacos:

- Corn or flour tortillas
- Shredded cabbage or coleslaw mix
- Sliced avocado
- Chopped fresh cilantro
- Lime wedges for serving

Instructions:

    Marinate the Shrimp:
- In a bowl, whisk together coconut milk, lime zest, lime juice, soy sauce, honey or maple syrup, minced garlic, grated ginger, salt, and black pepper.
- Add the peeled and deveined shrimp to the marinade. Allow it to marinate for at least 15-20 minutes.

    Cook the Shrimp:
- Heat coconut oil in a skillet over medium-high heat.
- Remove the shrimp from the marinade and cook them in the hot skillet for 2-3 minutes per side or until they are pink and opaque.

    Warm the Tortillas:
- While the shrimp is cooking, warm the tortillas in a dry skillet or microwave according to package instructions.

    Assemble the Tacos:

- Place a spoonful of shredded cabbage or coleslaw mix on each tortilla.
- Top with the cooked coconut lime shrimp.

Add Toppings:
- Add sliced avocado and chopped fresh cilantro on top of the shrimp.

Serve:
- Serve the coconut lime shrimp tacos with lime wedges on the side.

These coconut lime shrimp tacos are a burst of tropical flavors with the sweetness of coconut, the tanginess of lime, and the succulent taste of shrimp. Customize the toppings to your liking and enjoy this delightful and easy-to-make meal.

California Dreaming Smoothie Bowl

Ingredients:

For the Smoothie Base:

- 1 frozen banana, sliced
- 1/2 cup frozen berries (such as strawberries, blueberries, or raspberries)
- 1/2 cup frozen mango chunks
- 1/2 cup plain Greek yogurt or non-dairy yogurt for a vegan option
- 1/2 cup almond milk or any milk of your choice
- 1 tablespoon chia seeds (optional, for added texture and nutrition)

For Toppings:

- Sliced strawberries
- Blueberries
- Sliced kiwi
- Granola
- Shredded coconut
- Chopped nuts (such as almonds or walnuts)
- Honey or maple syrup for drizzling

Instructions:

Prepare the Smoothie Base:
- In a blender, combine frozen banana slices, frozen berries, frozen mango chunks, Greek yogurt, almond milk, and chia seeds.
- Blend until smooth and creamy. If the mixture is too thick, you can add more almond milk.

Assemble the Bowl:
- Pour the smoothie into a bowl.

Add Toppings:
- Arrange sliced strawberries, blueberries, sliced kiwi, granola, shredded coconut, and chopped nuts on top of the smoothie base.

Drizzle with Honey or Maple Syrup:
- Drizzle honey or maple syrup over the toppings for added sweetness.

Serve:
- Serve the California Dreaming Smoothie Bowl immediately.

This smoothie bowl is not only delicious but also packed with a variety of fruits, providing essential vitamins and nutrients. The combination of creamy smoothie base and crunchy toppings creates a delightful texture and flavor contrast. Enjoy this nutritious and colorful breakfast that captures the essence of a California dream.

Honey-Lime Grilled Chicken Skewers

Ingredients:

- 1.5 pounds boneless, skinless chicken breasts, cut into bite-sized pieces
- 1/4 cup honey
- Zest and juice of 2 limes
- 3 tablespoons soy sauce
- 2 cloves garlic, minced
- 1 teaspoon ground cumin
- 1 teaspoon paprika
- 1/2 teaspoon chili powder
- Salt and black pepper to taste
- Wooden skewers, soaked in water for 30 minutes

Instructions:

Prepare the Marinade:
- In a bowl, whisk together honey, lime zest, lime juice, soy sauce, minced garlic, ground cumin, paprika, chili powder, salt, and black pepper.

Marinate the Chicken:
- Place the bite-sized chicken pieces in a shallow dish or a zip-top bag.
- Pour the marinade over the chicken, ensuring it's well-coated. Marinate for at least 30 minutes to allow the flavors to infuse.

Preheat the Grill:
- Preheat your grill to medium-high heat.

Thread the Chicken:
- Thread the marinated chicken pieces onto the soaked wooden skewers.

Grill the Skewers:
- Grill the chicken skewers for 8-10 minutes, turning occasionally, until the chicken is fully cooked and has a nice char on the edges.

Baste with Marinade:
- While grilling, baste the chicken skewers with the remaining marinade for extra flavor.

Check for Doneness:
- Ensure the chicken reaches an internal temperature of 165°F (74°C).

Serve Warm:
- Remove the skewers from the grill and let them rest for a few minutes before serving.

Garnish (Optional):
- Garnish with additional lime wedges and chopped cilantro if desired.

These honey-lime grilled chicken skewers are a perfect balance of sweet, tangy, and savory flavors. They make a great main course for a summer barbecue or a tasty addition to your meal. Serve them with your favorite side dishes, such as rice, grilled vegetables, or a fresh salad, for a complete and delicious meal.

Sesame Ginger Quinoa Bowl

Ingredients:

For the Quinoa Bowl:

- 1 cup quinoa, rinsed and drained
- 2 cups water or vegetable broth
- 1 red bell pepper, thinly sliced
- 1 carrot, julienned or grated
- 1 cup broccoli florets
- 1 cup edamame (shelled)
- 2 green onions, sliced
- Sesame seeds for garnish
- Chopped cilantro for garnish (optional)

For the Sesame Ginger Dressing:

- 3 tablespoons soy sauce
- 2 tablespoons rice vinegar
- 1 tablespoon sesame oil
- 1 tablespoon grated ginger
- 1 tablespoon honey or maple syrup
- 1 clove garlic, minced
- 1 teaspoon sriracha or chili garlic sauce (optional, for heat)

Instructions:

Cook the Quinoa:
- In a medium saucepan, combine the rinsed quinoa and water or vegetable broth. Bring to a boil, then reduce the heat to low, cover, and simmer for about 15 minutes or until the quinoa is cooked and the liquid is absorbed. Remove from heat and let it sit, covered, for 5 minutes. Fluff the quinoa with a fork.

Prepare the Vegetables:
- Steam or blanch the broccoli florets and edamame until they are tender but still crisp. You can do this by boiling them briefly or using a steamer. Set aside.

Make the Sesame Ginger Dressing:

- In a small bowl, whisk together soy sauce, rice vinegar, sesame oil, grated ginger, honey or maple syrup, minced garlic, and sriracha or chili garlic sauce if using.

Assemble the Quinoa Bowl:
- In a large bowl, combine the cooked quinoa, sliced red bell pepper, julienned carrot, steamed broccoli, edamame, and sliced green onions.

Pour the Dressing:
- Pour the sesame ginger dressing over the quinoa and vegetables. Toss everything together until well coated.

Garnish and Serve:
- Garnish the quinoa bowl with sesame seeds and chopped cilantro if desired.

Serve Warm or Cold:
- Serve the Sesame Ginger Quinoa Bowl warm or refrigerate and serve it cold as a refreshing salad.

This Sesame Ginger Quinoa Bowl is not only delicious but also a great way to enjoy a variety of colorful and nutrient-packed vegetables. It's a versatile dish that you can customize with your favorite veggies or protein sources like tofu or grilled chicken. Enjoy!

California Zoodle Salad

Ingredients:

For the Salad:

- 4 medium zucchini, spiralized into noodles
- 1 cup cherry tomatoes, halved
- 1 cucumber, thinly sliced
- 1 bell pepper (any color), thinly sliced
- 1/2 red onion, thinly sliced
- 1 avocado, sliced
- 1/4 cup sliced black olives (optional)
- 1/4 cup crumbled feta cheese or goat cheese (optional)
- Fresh basil or cilantro leaves for garnish

For the Dressing:

- 3 tablespoons extra-virgin olive oil
- 2 tablespoons balsamic vinegar
- 1 tablespoon Dijon mustard
- 1 clove garlic, minced
- Salt and black pepper to taste

Instructions:

Prepare the Zoodles:
- Spiralize the zucchini into noodles using a spiralizer. Place the zoodles in a large bowl.

Add Vegetables:
- Add the halved cherry tomatoes, sliced cucumber, sliced bell pepper, sliced red onion, avocado slices, black olives (if using), and crumbled feta cheese (if using) to the bowl with the zoodles.

Make the Dressing:
- In a small bowl, whisk together olive oil, balsamic vinegar, Dijon mustard, minced garlic, salt, and black pepper until well combined.

Toss the Salad:
- Drizzle the dressing over the salad ingredients. Toss everything together until the vegetables and zoodles are well coated with the dressing.

Garnish:
- Garnish the salad with fresh basil or cilantro leaves.

Serve:
- Serve the California Zoodle Salad immediately as a light and nutritious meal.

This salad is not only vibrant and visually appealing but also a great way to enjoy a variety of fresh and crisp vegetables. The spiralized zucchini noodles add a fun and healthy twist to the dish. Feel free to customize the salad with your favorite vegetables and toppings to suit your taste preferences.

Citrus Avocado Salsa

Ingredients:

- 2 ripe avocados, diced
- 1 orange, segmented and diced
- 1 grapefruit, segmented and diced
- 1 small red onion, finely diced
- 1 jalapeño, seeds removed and finely minced
- 1/4 cup fresh cilantro, chopped
- Juice of 1 lime
- Salt and black pepper to taste

Instructions:

Prepare the Citrus:
- Cut the orange and grapefruit into segments, removing any seeds. Dice the segments into small pieces.

Dice Avocado:
- Dice the ripe avocados and place them in a large mixing bowl.

Combine Ingredients:
- Add the diced citrus segments, finely diced red onion, minced jalapeño, and chopped cilantro to the bowl with the diced avocados.

Squeeze Lime Juice:
- Squeeze the juice of one lime over the mixture.

Season:
- Season the citrus avocado salsa with salt and black pepper to taste.

Gently Toss:
- Gently toss all the ingredients together until well combined. Be careful not to mash the avocados.

Chill (Optional):
- For enhanced flavors, you can refrigerate the salsa for about 30 minutes before serving.

Serve:
- Serve the citrus avocado salsa as a topping for grilled chicken, fish, shrimp, tacos, or as a refreshing dip with tortilla chips.

This citrus avocado salsa is a vibrant and flavorful addition to your meals. The combination of sweet citrus, creamy avocado, and a touch of spice from the jalapeño creates a well-balanced and delicious salsa. Adjust the ingredients and spice level according to your preferences, and enjoy this refreshing salsa as a versatile accompaniment to various dishes.

Spaghetti Squash with Pesto and Cherry Tomatoes

Ingredients:

- 1 medium-sized spaghetti squash
- 1 cup cherry tomatoes, halved
- 1/2 cup basil pesto (homemade or store-bought)
- 2 tablespoons pine nuts, toasted (optional)
- Grated Parmesan cheese for garnish (optional)
- Salt and black pepper to taste
- Olive oil for drizzling

Instructions:

Preheat the Oven:
- Preheat your oven to 400°F (200°C).

Prepare the Spaghetti Squash:
- Cut the spaghetti squash in half lengthwise. Scoop out the seeds and pulp using a spoon.

Bake the Spaghetti Squash:
- Place the squash halves, cut side down, on a baking sheet.
- Bake in the preheated oven for about 40-45 minutes or until the squash is tender and the strands easily come apart with a fork.

Scrape the Squash:
- Allow the spaghetti squash to cool for a few minutes. Use a fork to scrape the flesh, creating spaghetti-like strands. Transfer the strands to a large bowl.

Combine with Pesto and Tomatoes:
- Add the halved cherry tomatoes to the bowl with the spaghetti squash strands.
- Spoon the basil pesto over the squash and tomatoes.

Toss and Season:
- Gently toss everything together until the spaghetti squash strands and tomatoes are evenly coated with the pesto.
- Season with salt and black pepper to taste.

Toast Pine Nuts (Optional):
- In a dry skillet over medium heat, toast the pine nuts until they are golden brown. Keep a close eye on them, as they can burn quickly.

Serve:
- Transfer the spaghetti squash mixture to serving plates.
- Drizzle with a bit of olive oil, sprinkle with toasted pine nuts (if using), and garnish with grated Parmesan cheese if desired.

This spaghetti squash with pesto and cherry tomatoes is a light and flavorful dish that's perfect for a healthy meal. The natural sweetness of the spaghetti squash combines well with the vibrant flavors of pesto and the freshness of cherry tomatoes. It's a great option for a vegetarian or gluten-free meal, and you can customize it with additional toppings or protein if desired.

California Citrus Chicken Salad

Ingredients:

For the Salad:

- 2 boneless, skinless chicken breasts
- Salt and black pepper to taste
- 1 tablespoon olive oil
- 6 cups mixed salad greens (lettuce, spinach, arugula, etc.)
- 1 cup cherry tomatoes, halved
- 1 avocado, sliced
- 1/2 red onion, thinly sliced
- 1/4 cup crumbled feta cheese or goat cheese
- 1/4 cup chopped fresh cilantro or parsley

For the Citrus Vinaigrette:

- 1/4 cup fresh orange juice
- 2 tablespoons fresh lemon juice
- 2 tablespoons extra-virgin olive oil
- 1 tablespoon honey or maple syrup
- 1 teaspoon Dijon mustard
- Salt and black pepper to taste

Instructions:

Grill the Chicken:
- Season the chicken breasts with salt and black pepper.
- Heat olive oil in a grill pan or on an outdoor grill over medium-high heat.
- Grill the chicken for 5-7 minutes per side or until fully cooked and juices run clear.
- Allow the chicken to rest for a few minutes, then slice it into thin strips.

Prepare the Salad:
- In a large salad bowl, combine the mixed greens, halved cherry tomatoes, sliced avocado, thinly sliced red onion, crumbled feta cheese, and chopped cilantro or parsley.

Make the Citrus Vinaigrette:

- In a small bowl, whisk together fresh orange juice, fresh lemon juice, extra-virgin olive oil, honey or maple syrup, Dijon mustard, salt, and black pepper until well combined.

Assemble the Salad:
- Drizzle the citrus vinaigrette over the salad ingredients.
- Add the sliced grilled chicken on top.

Toss and Serve:
- Gently toss the salad until all ingredients are well coated with the dressing.
- Serve immediately.

This California Citrus Chicken Salad is a burst of flavors with the sweetness of oranges, the tanginess of lemons, and the savory grilled chicken. It's a perfect light and nutritious meal for a refreshing lunch or dinner. Feel free to customize the salad with additional toppings or nuts for added texture and crunch.

Mango Coconut Chia Pudding

Ingredients:

- 1/4 cup chia seeds
- 1 cup coconut milk (canned or homemade)
- 1 ripe mango, peeled, pitted, and diced
- 1-2 tablespoons honey or maple syrup (optional, depending on sweetness preference)
- Shredded coconut and additional mango slices for garnish (optional)

Instructions:

- Prepare the Chia Seed Mixture:
    - In a bowl or jar, combine chia seeds and coconut milk. Stir well to make sure the chia seeds are evenly distributed in the liquid.
- Let it Set:
    - Cover the bowl or jar and refrigerate the chia seed mixture for at least 4 hours or overnight. This allows the chia seeds to absorb the liquid and create a pudding-like consistency.
- Blend the Mango:
    - In a blender or food processor, blend the diced mango until smooth. If the mango is not very ripe or if you prefer a sweeter flavor, you can add honey or maple syrup to the blender.
- Layer the Pudding:
    - Once the chia pudding has set, layer it with the mango puree in serving glasses or bowls.
- Garnish (Optional):
    - Garnish the Mango Coconut Chia Pudding with shredded coconut and additional mango slices for extra texture and flavor.
- Serve:
    - Serve the chia pudding immediately or refrigerate until ready to serve.

This Mango Coconut Chia Pudding is a delightful treat that combines the creaminess of coconut with the sweetness of mango. Chia seeds add a wonderful texture and pack a nutritional punch with fiber, omega-3 fatty acids, and various vitamins and minerals. Enjoy this tropical delight for a healthy and satisfying snack or dessert.

www.ingramcontent.com/pod-product-compliance
Lightning Source LLC
LaVergne TN
LVHW081556060526
838201LV00054B/1920